YOUNG QUEENS OF OLD KINGS

BY

Rakesh Bhasin

 pencil

ISBN 978-93-5610-950-6

© Rakesh Bhasin 2022

Published in India 2022 by Pencil

A brand of

One Point Six Technologies Pvt. Ltd.

123, Building J2, Shram Seva Premises,

Wadala Truck Terminal, Wadala (E)

Mumbai 400037, Maharashtra, INDIA

E connect@thepencilapp.com

W www.thepencilapp.com

DISCLAIMER: *The opinions expressed in this book are those of the authors and do not purport to reflect the views of the Publisher.*

Author biography

Born in Awadh, Rakesh Bhasin is a graduate in engineering from IIT Kanpur and a postgraduate from IIT Delhi. He also acquired an M Phil degree in Social Sciences from Punjab University. Besides engineering, the author has cultivated an interest in literature and word history. He has read extensively in Hindi, English, Punjabi and Urdu languages. Among his varied interests that include photography, music, fine arts, travelling and astrology, writing remains his passion. In the past, he has coauthored two volumes of selected stories of Munshi Premchand (abridged), a book titled 'Dastan-e-Awadh' based on life of Nawabs of Awadh and a book in Hindi language on the wondrous land of Meghalaya.

This book is another step in the literary journey of the author wherein he has shown classical legends through the lense of their female characters, giving them centre stage and louder voice.

You may reach him at r_bhasiniitk82@yahoo.co.in

Contents

Acknowledgements

I thank my daughter Mitali, a published author who was fortunately with us during most of the pandemic. She happily went through the multiple drafts of the book and rendered her professional advice.

Introduction

Legends come to us largely through folklores, from time immemorial. Some of them may have been born even before literacy and diction became a part of dialogue. These homespun accounts, stories and sagas, are believed by their narrators and listeners to have taken place sometime in human history.

This book is a collection of some of those stories. The accounts included in this book are events related to different times and are inherited from various civilizations. In fact, some of these are over three millennia old. The core of these stories has following features:

a) A stepmother, an old king's young queen, falls in love with her husband's chaste and pious son. The son is not her own but one born out of her husband's past marriage or affair. The primary reason of such forbidden advancement is the discontent on the part of a young queen, who has either been impelled to get married to an old king against her wishes, or is indignant towards the king's adulterous ways.

b) She offers herself to her husband's son, who finds it revolting and rebuffs her.

c) In her resentment for having been rejected, and her fear for ignominy, she plots against the son by falsely accusing him of making lewd advances towards her.

d) The king, believing the words of his young queen, takes severe action against his son and orders the son's death who dies painfully or barely escapes death.

e)   The king later becomes aware of the truth and realizes his blunder in judgment and repents bitterly.

I have included four legendary tales in this anthology. The first is the story of Loona, from Chamba[4], presently in province of Himachal Pradesh, India. Loona is a young low-caste maiden, married to King Salwan of Sialkot, now part of Pakistan. She is his second wife, married against her will, and is attracted to the King's adolescent son Pooran. Second is the story of Tishyrakshita, queen of Emperor Ashoka of the mighty Magadhan Empire, who is espoused as his fifth wife during the last phase of his life. She attempts to seek gratification from the young Prince Kunala. The third, the legend of Phaedra comes to us from Greek sources. Phaedra again is a disgruntled young queen of King Theseus of Athens who is allured towards the King's son Hippolytus. Lastly, this volume ends with the biblical account on the nameless, Potiphar's wife, from The Book of Genesis (Old Testament) who attempts to lure a young attendant in the household. The first three stories are tragedies and while the fourth ends happily.

I heard, for the first time, the legend of Loona and her obsession for her stepson Pooran during my study visit to Pangi Valley, a remote subdivision of the district Chamba, in Himachal Pradesh. This piqued my curiosity to pursue through various versions of the lore. Later, I searched over and found that similar stories existed in history, and legends of different civilizations. Thus began the journey of this book.

I discovered that in the classically recorded sagas, the young queens were portrayed as villains except in the modern day, the epic Loona by Shiv Kumar Batalvi, where Loona gets her voice. My present work is largely in the form of dialogues and is a departure from the medieval narratives and philosophies. I have shifted the rendition and shown to the readers these stories through the lens of their female characters. This book's female characters, unlike their folklore counterparts, get equal space where they divulge their inner feelings and ventilate their anguish. They aren't in remorse. They are bold enough to give expression to their desires and natural urges in a society that deplores female interest in sexuality, as lust. I hope I have been able to do partial justice with Loona, Tishyarakshita, Phaedra and Potiphar's wife through this work.

Each legend is followed by an epilogue to familiarize the reader about the various versions of the story, the background of its plot and social milieu that finds its reflection in the legend. I have provided endnotes elucidating the names of persons, places and mythical characters.

The miracles in the traditional scripts of the stories have also been excluded, making these sagas stand on firm ground to appeal to a rational mind.

Lastly, I must mention that this book is a product of the Covid-19 pandemic times, when entire world had to hide behind their masks and I was also mostly confined at home.

My search for more of such legends is still on and they will be added as we (I and my readers) explore them with the passage of time.

With these words, I place this work in your hands. I hope you would relish reading it as much as I enjoyed penning it.

Rakesh Bhasin
Jaipur

LOONA

Characters-I

SALWAN : King of Sialkot

VARMAN : King of Chamba

KUNT : Varman's wife, Queen of Chamba

LOONA : Low cast maiden of Chamba whom Salwan takes as his second wife

POORAN : Son of King Salwan

ICHCHARAN : First wife of Salwan, mother of Pooran

GOLI : Attendant of Ichcharan

BARU : Father of Loona

CHAUDHAL : King of Udhay, father of Ichcharan

IRA : Friend of Loona

MATHRI : Another friend of Loona

Loona-The Alluring Beauty

King Salwan is captivated by Loona's alluring beauty. The teenaged lass is strikingly charming with her delicate limbs, large bosom, pearly teeth, sleepy languid eyes, long hair falling till her ankles, fair and feisty. *Kamadev* [13] has played his trick on Salwan; the flame of desire has been kindled.

~

Salwan, the King of Chamba [4], was an honoured guest at Sialkot [29], in the palace of his friend, and sworn brother, King Varman. The occasion was Varman's birth anniversary celebration. The populace from common folks to the aristocracy of his kingdom came to join the religious rites. The King and his queen Kunt were readied by their entourage for the *mahayagna* [19] performed on the momentous day. The King was anointed with the choicest perfumes, essence of flowers, fragrant oils, bathed with water of holy river Ganges [7]. The Queen was also groomed with an equal dose of cosmetics prepared from natural herbs and flowers.

The arena was set. Flocks of black cocks and a hundred and twenty-one carefully selected sheep brought for the grand feast held after their sacrifice in the mahayagna. The Earth's face became deep red with the blood of the slaughtered creatures. The custom of applying the blood-red soil as a ritualistic mark on Varman's sunny forehead was performed by his sworn brother Salwan. The meat of the butchered animals was arranged in large vessels for cooking. A host of items were prepared for the feast. Amid the deafening sound of drums, trumpets, saxophones played by the musicians that filled the sky, a young girl from the gathering was chosen by King Varman to lead the prayer. The chosen charming maiden raised her delicate fair hands in front of the mother goddess, praying for the King's well-being and long-life. The King made the customary proclamation and declared himself the sworn father of the girl. She was showered with gifts, the title of land and a water-well. The name of this fortunate damsel was Loona. While all and sundry were engrossed in the excitement of the function, Salwan's eyes were soaked in the beauty of Loona. He was captivated by her at first sight at the arena. *Kamdev* [13] had successfully struck his arrow, hitting his heart instantly. It seems like the valorous kings were struck by *Kamdev's* arrow more frequently than those from their adversaries on battlefields. Back home at Sialkot, Salwan had Queen Ichcharan, his consort, and their eighteen-year-old son Pooran. Their existence; however, was far away from his mind, and heart, at that enchanting moment.

~

The ceremony has ended, leaving behind the fragrance of the previous day's festivity in the air. Silence that has overtaken the air is broken intermittently by the sweet chirping of birds and breeze rustling through the trees' leaves. The two royals are sitting in the palace's garden late in the morning. While Varman's face is beaming with contentment, Salwan's looks ruffled after a sleepless night. Loona's appealing playful face has not left his mind ever since he first saw her. His yearnings are making him increasingly restless.

Salwan's middle age is pricking him as teenaged Loona's face hangs around his eyes. The memory of the bygone blissful days of his youth haunts him as he speaks to Varman, "How ecstatic were those days! Truly ambrosial, as if a damsel is kissing her own roundness. But today that very fragrance has mutated like a harlot sleeping after a wakeful night's exertion."

Varman, while still lost in thoughts of the previous day's jamboree, nods, "Yes! My friend, some days are bright with sunshine while others are devoid of the sun. Bereft of all the fragrance, it is strange that yesterday was so different from today."

Salwan sounds mystical, "Oh my dear friend, the mighty King of Chamba! [4] Can anyone awaken the sleeping sun? Can anyone bring back yesterday's sun? We are not aware of what lies in the storehouse of destiny. My tongue hesitates. If I continue to shy away, my heart singes. If I speak my mind, I fear that I might lose my sun and its sunshine forever."

"Dear friend! Everyone is blessed with the sun as destined. Every sun is formative to shadow from the moment of its dawn. Even if the shadow eclipses your tongue today, I'm sure you'll not be deprived of its sunshine. Sunshine only dies when one stands in the shade or one's eyes are closed with slumber."

"Yes friend; I feel terribly drowsy. I intend to sleep in this broad day when the sun is at its zenith. I look to quench the heat of my sun. I am craving for a wink under the shadow of my own shade. As the time's yardstick removes my life's cloth measure by measure, I am dying to catch a hiatus. All of us are hankering for sleep, as we all are born in sleep and we die in sleep," says Salwan.

Varman adds, "You are right; we come to life in a sleepy amnesia and leave it in similar state. While we live there is no respite for us, as the cool shade we search for is effaced by the sunshine. But my dear friend, your lips have still not divulged the cause of your dejection."

Salwan now opens up a bit, "Oh dear! The only thing I can say; could a well that contains saline water ever become an oasis?"

"You continue to beat about the bush. After all, what is your distress? You understand well that sorrow is ephemeral, like sparrow it ever remains on wings, moving from one thatch to another."

Salwan croons, "Friend! Now I shall light the flame of my agony and touch it with my tongue. Let me take you around the city of my ill-fated sunshine, the dull flame of Chaudhal's hearth, Pooran's mother Ichcharan. Though she has been my daily inebriety, yet she could never possess my heart. She could never become my dream maiden. I struggled for long to burn my dream and erase my dream damsel's comely form from my memory's stream, but the more I writhed to brush the images aside, the more etched they became in my thoughts. Many a time, I thought of breaking the perfunctory bond and return Ichcharan back to her father's home. But I restrained myself, for her father's honour who has no fault. I passed my days monotonously, like a pebble in the river rolling at the mercy of the stream. I was born a radiant sun, but my life withered into a long dark night. I, however, never revealed my agony to her. She slept soundly by my side while I remained restless in bed. Then there appeared a moment of joy. On the leafless tree, a flower bloomed. I begot my son from her womb. But once again my misfortune followed me. I was advised by soothsayers not to see his face for eighteen long years. He was confined, and I slipped into a sea of darkness and morbidity again. I continued to be a slave of passion. If the meeting of our bodies remains bereft of touch of the divine, we breathe not as human but as a swine."

Varman replies, "I agree. Life without fire is like a fish out of water. Every fuel has to gulp flame to become fire. However, a flame remains a flame whether it blazes in the hearth or burns the pyre. If your Ichcharan happened to be an unripe fire you could have puffed or doused it from the very beginning. But, you must agree that the burning passion after indulgence leaves the taste of an unripe fire. Dreams continue to hang in our psyche upside down like bats. Our days roll on like a smouldering fire."

"Yes friend! Now when it's the twilight moment, the fuel of my sun is depleting fast. As the damsel of my dreams was fading away, I was suddenly face to face with her yesterday. I thought, for a moment, that destiny is again playing tricks with me…"

Varman joyfully interrupts, "Unbelievable! It is my fortune that my friend's dream comes true here. Please disclose who this matchless beauty is?"

"Yes friend! The one like the first ray of the sun, with sleepy languid eyes, ankle length hair, delicate limbs, milky fair, pearly teeth, Loona! Yesterday, chosen by you, to lead the prayers."

Varman shudders, "Loona…? The daughter of that low cast Baru? Beautiful, feisty, delicate indeed ….but born with the curse from previous incarnation, as if a fairy born defiled, like water of holy Ganges amidst wine. An outcaste woman can never attain the position of a consort of a King."

Salwan retorts, "If Loona is born to an untouchable, how is it her fault?"

"Fault? Fault is with her fortune or with her past lives," reasons Varman.

Salwan persists, "No! No! This is not her doing. It is our self-deception and our narrow religious understanding. Religion prompts us to blow conches in temples, to surrender to idols, to burn incense in front of stones, but when it comes to pouring a drop in the mouth of a dying human we shy away. We don't dither a moment when it comes to killing each other. And when time brings us to our own funerals, we raise monuments at our cremation sites adorning it with our own marble statues. What allegiance is this that doesn't recognize that all humans have the same colour of blood gushing through their veins? Truly speaking, we all are outcaste barbarians brimming with bigotry, rancor, falsity and hypocrisy creating artificial distinctions."

Salwan is immersed in his infatuation with Loona. On one hand, he has his reasons and logic as to why she shouldn't be made to suffer for being a low-caste untouchable, but refuses to look at his own cravings to marry a girl of his son's age. In matters of the heart, all cognitive abilities appear to get paralysed.

Varman can't see beyond set beliefs, and reasons with Salwan, "Our karmas are like poisonous snakes bred by us. They haunt us from birth to birth. There is no escape from them."

"These are not your utterings, but the expressions of your false belief that has been conditioned by the narrow religious commands."

Varman, still hopeful of his friend to reconsider, says, "Perhaps it is my delusion or my religious disorientation, but surely you are in a bout of intense physical lust. Your poisonous dream is discharging its expression through you."

"No! No! This is not lust my friend. I am not possessed by evil spirit. I am driven by my revolutionary makeup. Why is there so much hatred in the name of religion? Why doesn't man come out of this hazy notion of cycles of birth and death [6] ? I beseech you my friend to get me that girl as a wife."

Varman makes his last attempt, "My respectable friend, what is this you have uttered? You are stooping too low for that untouchable.

Please do not think of taking her as your wife. I may, however, arrange her for you if you agree."

Salwan in a strident tone, "No! No! That is not my desire. I have never sinned like that. I shall not indulge in it now. I desire her hand and companionship for this birth and beyond."

(Kunt, wife of King Varman, enters the chamber and addresses the king.)

Kunt with folded hands, "Greetings, my lord. I was listening to your entire conversation from behind the screen. I intend to submit, my lord, when sullied water meets the Ganges, it becomes holy. If Loona marries my dear brother how will she remain untouchable?"

Varman replies, "The mythical bird *chatak*[5] drinks only the first drop of rain, *swati*[30] . It never looks towards the Ganges. Its thirsty tongue never touches the Ganges, howsoever hallowed it may be. It is true that crows and cuckoos both are black but no crow is ever called a cuckoo."

"Of course, no crow can become a cuckoo but it raises the offspring of a cuckoo. If Loona becomes my brother's wife she may ignite his distinguished fire," Kunt again reasons.

"It is my wish also that his fire is kindled. But, I have a sense of shame and hesitation. What will be the reaction of people of Udhay[31] City? What will be the reaction of kin of Ichcharan? They might raise fingers."

Salwan cries out in impatience, "The blame will come to you after Salwan's breath has left his body!"

Varman's empathy nudges him say, "Yet I feel it would be unfair to cast away Ichcharan. She is the cool shade of your courtyard.

She is the mother of your son. When a woman has attained motherhood, she is like a mute cow. She must not be harmed."

Kunt argues without empathy, "A woman is a jewel to a man that he wears around his neck so long as she can win over his soul. If she fails, she can't be termed a woman. It is better for her to die and not to get birthed a woman again."

Varman reluctantly, "Kunt! A woman is a woman; it is an eye, which finds her charming. It is also an eye that beholds otherwise. All women are the fragments of Rati's[24] dream. Anyway, now that you both insist, convey to the minister to send a message to Baru's home for him to get ready for his daughter's marriage with my friend and get whatever he solicits."

(Isn't it ironic that one woman plays against another woman to get the scales tilted in the favour of the man.)

~

Loona Moves to Chamba

(Loona is married to Salwan. It is the month of May of Indian summers. Sitting in her bridal attire in a room of her home, she is conversing with her friends Ira and Mathri, before leaving for her in-laws'.)

Loona pours her heart, "I, the passion fire, am set to move to a distant destination. My breasts are twin infernos. I carry fire in one, and heat of this month of May in the other. When a passion fire comes of age, it is made to move to a far-off place. What kind of fate is she born with, that a father has to send the piece of his heart afar? When a young girl nears adulthood, her father loses his sleep, as if his courtyard is engulfed by flames. He desperately seeks for a suitable partner for her. Today it is my turn. Adorned with searing henna on my soles and donned in this burning bridal dress, I am to move to an alien land. But my dear friends, what kind of fire am I that while my eyes face the sun, a furnace is beneath my feet, my whole body singes as if I'm below the tree of fire, yet my own fire is abated, for the match my father has brought for me."

"Dear friend, don't utter such unseemly words. A woman is not meant to speak her mind. She is born mute, lives voiceless and fades away silently. If she dares open her mouth, she stands castigated and deserted by the society. She fritters away her life burning another's hearth, suffering veiled tears and muffled cries. Silence is the only virtue accredited to her since genesis. So please remember you are not to speak," replies Ira.

Loona retorts, "Ira, why should a woman remain so tongue tied? When she swallows such deep hurt, why should she not throw to winds all her restraints? Why doesn't all her forbearing not ablaze her into lightning and thunder, such explosive thunder that ruptures the eardrums of seven skies, bringing tremor in the *Ahiravan's*[1] underworld and all directions reverberating her agony? I wish that each hearth of every home must turn into an inferno torching all their limits. The tyranny buried in the pages of eternity must be exposed. The warmth of our fire should no more be weighed against a handful of millet given to us for our subsistence."

"My dear, your raging words suggest that you are under a spell of some witchcraft. It's a fact, that though being salty is a common metaphor for a belle, yet her own tears remain bereft of the taste of salt. Through ages, a woman is to live silently consuming her own tears…"

"Ira dear, my instinctive mind says that a day will come when every woman will break the shell and hiss fire. No more idle tears. She will abrogate the vanity of those who treat her as an object."

Ira vehemently opposes, "No! No! Do not foster such concocted notions. A woman's woeful destiny is unalterable. Every mother, therefore, professes her daughter to seek a remote dark corner of the house to spin the wheel of her sufferings, with nobody sensing even an inkling of her sorrow."

Loona persists, "Ira my sister listen; how can one rip off the ghost of such fabricated beliefs? These are not the trees, which can be sawed and felled. The superstitions have chained our delicate feet, in the name of modesty. Shackled under the load of professed good conduct we, the obedient beings, suffocate; reeling from one birth to another carrying gibbet on our shoulders meekly surrendering to the misplaced notion of a make-believe hell and heaven."

"This is a game of destiny that one cannot evade, Loona…."

Loona interrupts, "If there is something called destiny it emanates as the melody through one's own actions. Human dignity lives only in action."

Mathri intervenes, "Loona! It is hard to seek, why your heart is under the dark shadow of melancholy. You are fortunate to get an ideal man who has elevated you from dust to the throne. Do not speak low of him, he who has mutated you from an ordinary puddle to the water of holy Ganges. Reflect upon if you even deserve him. Have you ever imagined sun perambulate around an earthen lamp? It is your great luck that your husband is a King."

Loona bitterly, "To me, a low-born, bring a low-born groom. Take away all these flowers and place thorns on my way. Seize the palace, its lofty attics and give me a humble hutment. Please set me within the bricks of its walls. A wild marigold is any day desirable to a weathered, fragrance-less jasmine. Where there is no harmony of age, the fluid of two bodies when mingles does not metamorphose into Ganges. I prefer to remain a low caste cobbler than to be the queen of a worn-out king. Burning coal from a hearth is better than the dowsed fire from a sacred altar."

Friend Mathri questions, "But why don't you see that old musk is much more valuable than fresh asafetida?"

"Asafetida is certainly better than the fabled musk. Can asafetida ever be demeaned as lesser to musk?"

Mathri muttered, "No! No! I cannot demean. I am one like you who feels the pain, the agony of a woman."

"Listen my dear friend! Is there anyone who can truly feel a woman's pain and agony? When a girl is born, her mother is in tears, for every mother dreams for a son. On seeing the face of the girl her milk dries up. The colour of a father's turban also fades, and its crest is lowered. He feels letdown. From the day of her birth he carries the anxiety to send her away."

Mathri tries to pacify Loona, "As one lamp lights another, dear friend; a life originates through another. Only a woman has the power to create, and a creator cannot be annihilated even by the cruel hands of death. Days, years, centuries roll, but the creative energy never ceases. It lives on forever."

"Is it honest to say that a woman is a creator? When a fire of passion is lit, and the craving of the flesh is gratified, the fruit naturally appears on the fictitious branch of love. It is all for the momentary impulse that an idol of flesh and blood sprouts....And when compulsion is dubbed as creation, she is only to laugh at herself."

Ira attempts to elevate Loona's sagging spirits, "It is the feminine energy that shapes whatever enchanting exists on Earth. She is the touch of divine. She is the intuitive third eye that ornate every being. A woman is the living ballad of the mother earth. A family's lineage cannot perpetuate without her. The most alluring dimension of a woman's persona is her potential for a covert liaison; every other thing is just ordinary. She, however, keeps her passions under lock of an ideal dream, which never comes true. As time rolls, the lock getting withered and rusted breaks on its own, shattering all the dreamy ideals."

Loona wails bitterly, "Dear doves...! Put a lock on me that can never be opened, and never be broken. Shatter my ivory bangles and burn all my bridal adornments. Tell my sire to bring the palanquin, to take away this dead fire to Kot Sial[18]."

Ira helplessly, "O the daughter of Chamba do not cry! Had it been a piece of jaggery[12]we could have shared it with you. But how might we share your sorrow? Please do not shed tears."

Mathri emotively, "Ira, let her cry and wash away the wounds of her heart. Tears bring some relief to our sorrows; let her tears lighten the burden of her heart. If tears do not trickle down women's eyes, the whole world might go mad burdened with grief. Tears are our selfless comrades; very silently, they flow for the sake of our agony. Friendship of one tear is more comforting than the friendship of a hundred lovers. In the game of love, a loser has an edge over the winner."

(Loona's father Baru enters the room.)

Baru emotional, with a lump in his throat speaks, "The pain of a daughter's heart can only be felt by her mother. A father is unable to fathom its depth. People rightly say that poverty is more like a *Narsimah Avatar[21]*,it neither strangles inside, nor slays on the outside, it kills at the threshold. A daughter's birth in a poor man's home is a curse…. My lovely bird; the palanquin bearers are ready; the King himself awaits with his horsemen, all set for Kot Sial. Take away your sire's love for one last time."

Baru addresses Ira, "Ira dear, you accompany Loona and be with her like a shadow for a few days. Take good care of her and return to Chamba when she feels at home there. Keep remitting the message of her wellbeing through someone."

(With a farewell song on lips of the girls, everyone leaves.)

~

Ichcharan-The Queen of Chamba

(Ichcharan received the news of King Salwan's second marriage. Sitting in her palace with her maid companion Goli, she is lamenting.)

"O father dear, which land have you given your daughter to, where people don't spare a thought towards the pain of a woman, where the evil omened sun rises with no affinity even to its own sunshine. In this beastly jungle, fair are snared and abused. Trees are simply bare without a flower or fruit. Here sale and purchase of flesh is an everyday pursuit, and a woman is treated no more than footwear."

"O Queen, be patient, do not lose heart. Expecting fidelity from a man is like asking for a ray of light on a new moon night," consoles Goli.

Ichcharan with a deep sigh, "I am not asking for loyalty from him, my dear simpleton. I am merely yearning for my death. My heart is sinking, my tongue is twisted. I am breathless. It is a humiliating moment that the king has married an untouchable. Hold! My heart just missed a beat."

"Where is the surprise in the king falling for a low born? These hedonistic men ever look to closet with harlots. A woman for them is a thing of momentary use. She loses all her charm to a man after his indulgence. Caring about her caste may be an afterthought for him. A telling relationship cannot be expected from a man. There is a stark divergence in their conduct during the day, and in the night. They change colour like a chameleon."

"I do understand chameleons' changing colours but I can't gauge the changing nature of men. I can measure the sting of a deadly viper but can't fathom the bite of a man," bitterly said Ichcharan.

"O Queen! I wonder for the kind of fate written for women. Destiny sharpens the teeth of the saw, every day, to rip off the sandal tree that women are. Remaining in captivity of men's heartless will, women even return whatever gains they make in life's gamble, to their wicked, miserly gamblers. Even dogs are better creatures, who get stale bits of food, yet remain loyal to their masters. But the men, in the name of love, continue to lust around at other doors for stolen affairs. They eat at one door during the day and sleep at another during the night," replied Goli.

"My compatriot, I the sunshine, supplicate to return my sun to me. I, the daughter of Udhay City[31], beg with the folded hands that even if you squeeze the fire out of my limbs, slaughter me into pieces and throw me into stream, I cannot repudiate my duties. It is beyond the psyche of an Indian woman to wipe out the sacramental vermillion off her forehead. Her husband remains her God, forever. I am aware of all their vices; you need not recount them to me. Let us not open their failings. We go to the temple, lighting lamps in front of a deity and silently accept whatever requital we get."

"You live under plain simple blind faith. Closing your eyes and deceiving your mind. This way, the women of this land would never be redeemed from centuries of sorrow and disdain," contends Goli.

Ichcharan reiterates, "Woman is another name of 'blind faith'. A woman and her tender feelings are like a wound and its pain. One cannot be separated from the other."

"If this is your belief then why shed tears for Salwan? Let him marry a thousand Loonas. Ignore and do not scream."

Ichcharan bemoans, "No Goli, it is not my belief. What row could an ordinary woman like me begin? For one, who could not captivate her husband by her charm, no one else is to be blamed. Even when a tamed bird flies away, it is deeply agonizing. When one's husband drifts away, how can one sit back or sleep? The body turns listless, as if it is just a lump of flesh and bones. No one can share my grief; neither do I feel like airing it. My heart is devastated like wilderness, overrun and desolate. I have a feeling like the blistering hot wind blowing at noon in the month of May singe my body, turning my complexion to copper. As if I am faced with a vast stretch, of barren land without a tree, simply dotted with odd shrubs, burning pyres, with hovering vultures, wind blowing with hiccups and in spooky silence witches follow. A sudden knock breaking the eerie silence, sends shivers down the spine. Someone go and tell Salwan that this macabre hush is devouring me. The wailing of dogs can be heard through my ominous soul, and I am afraid of my own self. Please plead him, for the sake of Pooran, to show me his face at least once."

Goli vies, "It is all mandated by one's jinxed fate that one is confined to the darkness of a grave on a broad day. We women have lost our dignity by willingly supplicating to men. The moon's image may appear mesmeric in a calm lake but one cannot catch it by simply entering the lake. It is my humble plea to women that a man be constrained to pledge his entire estate before she shares a hint of her fragrance with him. She should not be carried away by his sweet deceptive words unless he learns to obey. O Queen, please do not waste your tears, nor fold your fair delicate hands to the devil whom you delusively regard as your God. O Queen, of this land, why do you dissipate your life for a liar who knows only the taste of flesh? The men in the guise of God rob guileless women of their innocent dreams."

"Sarma[26] was a bitch at Lord Indra's[10] door. We are nothing more at the doors of our men. We bless them for our day's bread and shade of their roof over us to sleep. We are like moccasins in the feet of men, whether we fit in them or not is our kismet. If I were barren, I would not have kept a grudge. I have illuminated his courtyard, but there is no indemnity to me for the pain I have undergone. My son Pooran is confined and my husband has been snatched away. My fortune has forsaken me. I know not where to go, I have lost my way. Leaving Pooran confined to the underground cave, and moving to my parents doesn't seem appropriate. Return of a married daughter to her parents is seen in bad light. They will lose face. People would say how tactless I am to have managed my life so poorly."

"O Queen, men do not think of progeny, they just hunt women for their sensual fulfilment. *Kamdev's* offspring, every man filled with poison, bites the woman impelled by his carnal cravings. And the woman fondly carries the offshoot of his debauchery, the fruit of his poison, in her womb. Inebriated by motherly affection, her spirit soars above the empyrean heights deceiving herself in the name of faithfulness. O Queen, lust and faith are things pole apart. Faith is a pleasing aroma emanating from the flowers. Faith is like the colour of jasmine mingled with sunlight. And a woman is like the mythical *chakor[3]* enamoured by the moon, who mistakes fire for the moon and burns her plumes. If an earthen pot breaks, it is dumped in a junk pile. When a woman's life breaks, she has to go back to her parent's home. The one who creates life is laughed at by the world."

Ichcharan thoughtfully, says, "O Goli! Estranged lovers might come around but no one can reconcile with an alienated wife. She turns into fire in a bamboo forest that cannot be extinguished even by the torrential rain. The entire world on one side cannot subdue an enraged wife. But Goli, I can't even afford to be estranged. In whose care shall I leave my Pooran? I waited for eighteen years of his protracted confinement. Now when the tree is nearing bloom, how do I abscond from him? If I had no motherly affection for my son, I would have left Salwan's Kingdom. A woman can bear the agony of separation from her husband, but not from her son. A creeper can survive without roots, but not without leaves. Without her son around, a woman is washed-up like a line drawn on water's surface. I know there are women with their lusterless skin, made-up by rubbing acacia bark, who lure stale men with their wily smiles. Even King Dasratha[15]lost his sense of reason and banished Ram to forest, for the machinations of a woman who wished to secure the throne for her son Bharat. Whenever I remember my son, Goli, I am shaken up from the inside. My heart beats like a tambourine, my head splits, my belly singes, my tongue becomes parched and my breath gets choked in my throat. I get skeptic of Loona and her tricks. Women from the hills are experts in magic and witchcraft. Men who come in close touch with them, their restless soul wanders for several births. If such a woman takes fancy of a man, she ventures him out of his grave to satiate her urge. I think I must arrange for Pooran's marriage once he is out of the custodial cave. I shall paint the heads of musical drums with my own hands for ceremonial ballads, shall distribute sweets and apply henna on Pooran's hands. I shall select a fairy for him, but then all this appears merely my fancy's flight. When misfortune makes its way in a courtyard, happiness of a home bids adieu. May Loona and her Salwan live long. My setting sun has lost its heat. A part of my life is already over….rest shall pass somehow. I shall not grumble, nor shall I say a word to Salwan. My nights will pass turning sides. I shall swallow the sweet poison of separation."

Goli says humbly, "O my beloved Queen! I can no more see you in grief. I have lived on your salt. My heart rends watching your treacherous destiny. Allow me to present a suggestion. You should go to your parents for few days. With change in weather, you might feel better. Sitting detached in loneliness adds to sorrow. A patient feels a tad better by turning sides. Having a dip in the Ganges may not wash away our sins but it may ease us of our delusions. You need not worry for your son. He is like my own. There are still five months to go before Pooran comes out of his confinement. I assure to keep enquiring about him every day. I carry an anxiety like a mother for him in my heart."

"Go O Goli! Ask the charioteer to get the chariot ready immediately, for my journey to Udhay City. The creeper nurtured in Salwan's courtyard is to be uprooted and destroyed. The dark boat of my life laden with my grief be drowned."

(Ichcharan sobs inconsolably. Goli leaves the room.)

~

The Young Queen & The Prince

(Pooran is out of prolonged confinement, staying in Loona's palace for few days. Loona engaged in sharing her grief with her friend Ira, sitting on the terrace. The air is moist with mild drizzle.)

Loona goes on incessantly, "O dear friend! What kind of days are these, rain soaked and languid? Dark-dense clouds have arrived as guests. A while ago, there was sun in the garden, and now it has gone. It hopped, and smiles over the temple dome now. Some time ago, the sky was bursting with laughter, and now tears well up in its eyes. Lightening popped up like a necklace in the sky, now it frightens like a serpent. The peacock screamed aloud in the jungle, now a blackbird is shedding tears over the tree. A while ago, a jubilant songbird was humming, now a nightingale plays a wistful tune. Herons soared in dark clouds like flowers over the cloud tree. White lotuses are floating in the lake. The Earth that appeared washed and clean, now it spreads its messy hair. A string of herons just flew past, appearing like a plaited garland Earth put around the sky's neck in devotion. Dear friend, just now, I thought to myself about how wonderful it would be to die at this moment. They say, one who dies during the rains becomes a cold dusky cloud and is never born again on Earth. But I am not so fortunate, my friend, even to greet my death at this moment. May your friend Loona turn into a roving cloud and fade away drop by drop. I am at a loss of my wits; I have lost my way to myself. Loona today stands aloof from her own self. She stands in the middle of a jungle on fire. Every nook of it harbours flowers of fire mingling their fragrance with fire. An odd butterfly of fire hovers over the flowers of fire. All ten directions are blowing fire and only fire…. But in this jungle of fire, Loona stands numb and frozen. O friend!

I intend to make a confession….whenever I look at Pooran, I feel as if an ode is flowing through me. I begin breathing and exuding sandal. My heart turns into a cheerful deer park, where a musk exuding fire-deer gallops and sprints. But when a leaf of discretion falls, this deer of fire looks away. How do I restrain this deer of my fire? Should I make it blindfolded or fasten it with the pin of modesty. The garden does not enchant it, neither does it like the cool shade of palaces or prefer the cozy bed of the King. It detests the grass of gold but the deer of fire craves to eat burning coal…. And it is dying for Pooran."

Ira is dazed, "Loona! What did you just utter? What is this all about fire-deer and a jungle of fire? What do you desire from Pooran?"

Loona, "I want fire for my fire-deer."

Ira tries to counsel, "You want fire? What nonsense is this you babble? Isn't it a forbidden fire? In the body of that fire, you don't seem to feel the reflection of your own body's heat. His mouth not only has fragrance of Ichcharan's milk, but yours too. Though you both match in age yet, dear friend, your womb is the shadow of his mother's womb. Loona, I caution you in all earnestness, never to touch this forbidden fruit. Think of Pooran as your own son. Never desire to have a union with him. Better to sell your fire-deer to a butcher to skin it alive. Please do not bring Chamba and your father to disrepute."

Loona remains inexorable, "Ira, you sermon me with strange logic. You rub salt on my bare wounds. You have no pity on me that my father committed a grave sin by marrying me to a wilted flower, used up by Ichcharan. I, of Pooran's age, have become his mother. I am just a kiss older than him. How could I be his mother when he wasn't born through my womb? …. And friend, I am like a daughter to Salwan. People aren't ashamed, if a father consumes the beauty of a daughter. But, if a Loona falls in love with a Pooran the world feels appalled. Yes, I may be characterless if I traded my smile. But, if parents can't find a matching suitor for their daughter, what is the sin if she chooses one herself? Loona stands guilty if she was solemnized with Salwan from her heart? My fragrance continues to be of a virgin. Therefore, dear friend, do not waste your advice on me, as you know not the anguish of my heart. I am unable to admit this relationship. It is a capricious relation between two unequal fires. Fire is meant to inflame and illuminate. Fire only can kill my fire deer. Young age knows no other relation. Friend, when my golden body approaches the bridal bedstead it exudes a foul odour. Don't you understand the restlessness of that moment? Feel of the instant is loftier than high heavens, soaked with ethereal fragrance, drowned in the sea of intoxication. But I abhor Salwan's bed…his touch. Whenever that moment is afire a snake creeps over my head. At that blazing moment I cry, I laugh feverishly. In the jungle of fire-flowers, starkly naked, I dance. I break away from my own shadow. I feel blinded, yet I see everything. Like a pregnant viper, I bite my own self. In every day's broken mirror, I see my own poison-smeared face. Every image laughs at me and I mock every face. I plunge over the contours of my own face. But, I find these high contours stretch endlessly and I turn breathless climbing over them. These walls cry for me and I cry for them. Night after night, Loona loses her identity. My own face does not fit my body. In the crowd of my swarming faces, I have lost my original facade. Every moment of the day hinges heavy and restless. The foul smell of my smoldering heart lingers. Mute silence sings the elegy of my life. Loona mocks Loona, and Loona shies away from Loona. At every dawn, Loona rolls her spinning wheel and spins the rays of sun. As the day sets, she hangs herself from the ceiling of life with the rainbow rope. But, death doesn't come to her, she has been hanging in a void since eternity. The Earth has slipped under her feet and the sky above has cracked, Loona and her clay are falling apart."

"Loona! It is imminent for the clay to disintegrate from the being someday, yet we do carry on. Every woman on the Earth shares her fate with Loona. Love deceives every courtyard. Every woman remains in the state of suspended self-sacrifice. She neither lives nor dies. Every man here is like Salwan, an insult to every Loona's dignity. Here a woman is traded cheap, while bread is prized dearer. Here women are burnt in the hearth of every house. This is a city of dead, where no one divulges one's own grave but everyone mocks at others' death. Here everything is weighed against a morsel of bread. Here bread is a substitute for love, virtue and one's good conduct. Here bread only stands for wisdom, learning and skill. Date, day and festival are all metonyms of bread. In the city where bread is a beloved, Loona has to become a mother of Pooran, for bread's sake. What else are you seeking in this land? Why are you trying to cover your nakedness in this land of nudes? Unclad, you look one with others. Just strangle the fire-deer that races in your blood. A woman buries her luminous tree in her father's courtyard and brings her shadow for her husband. Loona, bury your dreams deep within yourself. Countless Loonas perish here every day this way. Satiating other's dreams, one day a life sprouts from her womb. In the shade of the plant she loses the sight of all her pains."

"Ira, your thinking is bizarre. The dream of a girl's father's home never sleeps, it always breaths in her subconscious. Friend, when a daughter reaches her simmering adolescence she fondles with a pristine dream *'she is playful in a jungle teeming with flowers in the company of her friends. Suddenly, she realizes that she is marooned. Not finding her friends after frantically searching, exhausted she seeks respite under the shade of a tree. Then a beautiful prince from the land of fairies appears. He takes her around the forest for a while. Days roll, and then a day comes when he marries the girl and takes her to a far-off country. Singing and laughing they spend their days merrily thereafter. Deeply in love, they wouldn't bear even a moment of separation. But, a dream is a dream…a demon appears in place of the prince. He marries her and puts her in a dark room. He eats her up every night, bit by bit. The dream she had woven in her father's home gets shattered. The dream she saw had the image of someone like Pooran. It keeps floating day and night in her eyes.* 'Ira, I feel that Pooran and I are the companions of previous births. We were one soul that was separated, for some curse. I lost him and he lost me. I am the destination of Pooran's search. I am the fragrance of his limbs. I am the wine dripping off the melodic words from Pooran's mouth. I am the flame of the sun that shines on Pooran's forehead."

Ira nods saying, "Yes Loona, every human with lose ideals pretends the same way. Every craving mortal preys after a love-filled being. A Pooran is every Loona's dream. But this is illusive like a mirage. We all are helpless, disgruntled, paltry beings. Through generations, we have mastered the art of outsmarting one another for lust and thirst."

(Rain drenched Pooran enters the terrace. Ira walks away. Pooran's milky white clothes are sticking to his body. Loona throws an amorous glance towards him. Pooran greets with folded hands.)

Loona smilingly, "Pooran! The weather is quite enchanting today."

"Yes mother, as if a lovelorn lassie is shedding tears."

Loona sweetly, "Yes Pooran! You described it correctly. This season is laden with tears, sad with pangs of separation. While Lord Indra was creating seasons, he fell deeply in love with a fairy, Ender. He chose the flavour of each season, basing it on her fluctuating moods. It is said that when she laughed it was spring, when she became fervent with passion he created summer, her lassitude prompted him to conceive autumn, when she danced with the jingling anklets pre-winter arrived, the chilly winter was born of her exhaustion, and the sixth rainy, the season of malhar[20]that stands today like that damsel soaked in the pain of separation. Ender was married to someone else and cried in the throes of separation from Indra. They say that Indra became dead-drunk on that day and crafted this season. Whenever Indra's heart becomes heavy with the memories of Ender, he weeps and there is downpour from the sky."

Pooran genially, "Revered mother, you narrated a very sweet tale that trickled a scent of separation from the clouds. It's as if incessant tears of Indra are descending as raindrops."

Loona with a mischievous smile says, "But Pooran, you haven't noticed your own Ender. You have dwelled in her heart for many births, but you don't seem to remember her. But whenever your Ender misses you she becomes a lovelorn damsel and even these raindrops remain unequal to her tears."

"Mother dear, which Ender you are referring to? Are you making fun of Pooran?"

Loona tries to be earnest, "Pooran, it is not jesting. There is no story more moving than this. Ender lives in an obscure and unapproachable land, where the sky lies below the feet and the Earth is seen overhead. She lives there all alone, fed on your memories, bearing with her swaying moods. She passes her day sitting over a mound singing all the way in an inaudible tone. She is an untouchable, though married yet remains an untouched virgin."

"Yes dear mother, I have understood your mythical tale of some fairy-land."

"Pooran, it is not one of those stories from the fairy land. You are not aware of that poor girl's plight. I wish she could come here to you. She would have arrested you in her eyelids. She would have danced merrily over the burning coal for your sake. She meets you only in her dreams. She joyfully laughs in her incorporeal frame seeing your blooming limbs. She pays obeisance at your door every day but returns with tearful eyes. At times, she visits my place, cries talking about you. That is a song that cannot be sung, a body that cannot be touched, a shadow that cannot be seen and a feeling that cannot be described…it's a script-less story, with pages afloat without a beginning, middle or end."

"Mother dear, please leave the story now and tell me who that aggrieved girl is?" asks Pooran curiously.

"Pooran! I am not aware of her name. Someone of her age addresses her as mother and the one who is like her father calls her his wife."

(Loona starts crying. Pooran now takes her clue.)

"But mother, what else should Pooran address her if he doesn't call her mother," says Pooran warily.

Loona replies lusciously, "Like a split tongue snake, from one tongue he should address her mother and beloved from another."

Pooran in a didactic tone, "That girl doesn't seem to have regard for Pooran. If she is ashamed of being called a mother, then she has no right to be a beloved. Because every beloved's face subtly, contains a mother and every mother's face subsumes the face of a beloved. The woman who lacks the sense of motherly affection is not a woman in any way. She has a limited womanhood and is yet to grow as a woman. As she is neither a mother, nor a sister, nor a beloved, she has no right to love."

"Pooran, Loona has deep respect for motherly love but she is wary of the affection which is thrust upon her womb. That kind of motherhood no woman would like. A woman dreams of the motherhood that sprouts out of love with a man. Pooran! Loona envisions motherhood through your limbs. Loona carries the fragrance of your body into hers. She has seen the shadow of your face in her womb. That image is conceived within Loona many a time taking form and blood and taking birth. I get ecstatic seeing the small tender limbs of the divine image that sleeps over my breasts. You become his father and I the mother."

"Mother, don't you see me as an extension of that tender image? Don't you find in me the fine grown up form of that same delicate shadow of your fantasy? Don't you sense the same affection for Pooran, which you find in that divine image?"

Loona reasons, "Pooran! I see only Pooran in Pooran and no Loona there. Pooran[23] to me remains *apooran²* without Loona. Pooran appears to be only a part of that image."

"Mother! Please become the mother of the slice of Pooran in which you see your reflection and you provide your cool shade. Listen O dear Mother! How can Pooran expose his heart's anguish? No words can match his agony and pain after being condemned to lonely seclusion for eighteen long years. Seasons came and wasted away for him. What was the outcome of that travail? The snakes of his father's misdeeds stung the feelings of Pooran chilling his remaining emotions. Those who gave birth to Pooran threw him on the streets, practically like an orphan. Not finding a mother at home, the home became an alien place for him. Mother left to her father's place leaving him without the shade of her affection. Since the day of his birth, Pooran is devoid of all happiness in his life," Pooran continues to pour out his heart, "He is wrecked by a host of tragedies. Firstly, he is burning under his own fire. Secondly, the misfortune of his mother breaks his heart. Thirdly, he is scared of the dark shadow of his father's black deeds. Lastly, from today the shelter of your courtyard has also been inhibited for him. Within these four walls, I feel suffocated. Pooran will quit these boundaries now. He will dissolve in the clouds, diffuse in breeze, nest in flowers, merge with sunrays, descend with shade, become one with eternity. Mother, here every house is on ruinous fire. But, no one has eye that can see each-other's house on fire. Everyone here is lost, but is shying away to ask the way to one's own home. Everyone dies here unlamented on the crossroad on a chilly night of one's life. Loona, here everyone spits blood like you and me…And the one who is an exception is a stone, not a human being."

"Pooran! I only intended to show you the way to your home but that perhaps is not agreeable to you. I aimed to divvy each-other's pain. But you don't seem to value my love."

"Mother, here no one has love for anyone. Here only one body meets another with no reverence for souls. Here everyone is scared of others during the day and gets scared of oneself as the night descends. Whirling around the grindstone, everyone is deceiving oneself, obsessed with fatal narcissism. Every custom here is ostentatious, love is superficial and morality is pseudo. Here everyone is seething with lust; the wind that blows is laden with lust. Everyone here is in a mad rush to outplay others. Everyone here is crippled, yet trying to debilitate others. Scared of one's own inner quietness, everyone hankers for a company. Everyone here is dancing naked, shying away from oneself. Everyone is licking poison, digging one's own grave, and hanging on his own gibbet. The moments of past, present and future here have fallen into the abyss. The three-tongued snake of time has already stung itself. Now the Earth stands still. What is left is a pallid darkness."

Loona persists, "Pooran, this is nothing but your vanity. Even today, if you split a ray of light it breaks into the same seven colours. But, everyone like you has eyes but no vision. No colour has faded but we can't see them, for our own blindness and depleted gusto. Dissect Loona, you'll find all colours vibrant with each colour having its own history, each one having its own fragrance. It is the tragedy with colours, that whenever two colours are blended, both lose their identity and a new colour is born. Continue mixing them and the hues go on changing. When seven colours mingle, they become the sunshine. But, the cruel hands of destiny at my father's place has turned my colours murky. The colours were weighed against the hunger of Loona's poor father. I desire a third colour that mixes with the two and gives birth to a new colour to this drab courtyard. May Loona's colourless body be dyed in your colour and renew the mood of this forlorn house."

"You want the third colour to lose its identity in the mix of other two? Loona, these are the shades of destiny. They get matched or wiped out, steered by what has been imprinted on our foreheads from day one."

Loona turns haughty, "Pooran, in the colours of Loona you mix your deep red colour...Lest Loona burn all the colours of this house, obliterating your colour before making every hue of this story pallid."

"Whatever Loona desires, she may go ahead with. It seems better that Pooran dies colourless. My blood may be used to provide a new coat on the dull and drab walls of this house. But I can't imagine trading the heat of my colours with my mother."

"If you can't sell your heat, I will sell my shade. I have lived without the sun, now I shall try and live even without the shade," scathingly says Loona.

Pooran replies calmly, "Mother, love means paying respect to each other's spirit. Love is never a perfunctory mix and match of colours. To obliterate one colour by another is no love but carnality. Loona, love resides in the eyes of beholder; it never surfaces on the lips. Love is the saga of silence, it is never a loud assertion. Love is an incense simmering within, without showing its warmth outside. Loona, you are afflicted by your lust. Pooran would have shared the love, if love were apparent in Loona. Your profound love would have surely made its presence felt. Though I feel sad for your ordeal, yet I don't have a cure for it. It was better if you were not born or I would have died at birth."

(Pooran leaves. Loona continues to cry on the terrace alone.)

~

King's Indiscretion

(Loona and Salwan are having leisure time in the Royal Gardens as the sunsets. Salwan lost in Loona's love, conversing with her.)

Salwan looks enamoured, "Loona! Today's setting sun is hypnotizing, as if a butterfly dancing in a crimson saffron field. Milky white clouds, like drubbed raw cotton, float in the sky. Sun appears like a golden pot floating in a stream of colours. The sun has risen and set earlier too, but never had such conspicuous bright colours. It is your company's magic that the days have become honey soaked, flowers sweetly scented and trees turned lusciously green. Breeze filled with a wine-soaked fragrance wafts whole day. Every season is filling its beak with your fragrant breath. Every day the fire instrument plays a passionate tune, with your lips humming fervent melody over some playful lyrics. It appears that a masterly sculptor has carved your limbs out of a dusky marble. The fine fragrance of your body is so intoxicating as if a sandalwood forest is in flames. Such is the bewitching company of yours that makes every night short as if it ends before the day falls. My days were different without you. They were absolutely desolated. My dawns were without warmth, moonshine was grimly patchy and I was completely adrift. In the jungle of despondency, I was like a marooned deer, thirsty through births in the quest of water of your beauty. I remained forlorn even amidst the merriments and festivities. I was like a lamp burning in the graveyard at sunset. Ghosts of unknown fears kept following me. A shadow of queer stillness pierced my bones. I walked not on the surface of the Earth, but below it. I repeatedly tried to rise above the Earth, but couldn't find a way and remained suffocated. But Loona, today your Salwan again walks the Earth, without a hint of despair. Loona, I ask from God now nothing else, but your eternal company."

(An attendant hurriedly makes entry.)

Attendant hastily says, "Your Majesty! If my life is spared may I submit something?"

"Go ahead! What do you want to say?"

"Blessed, your Majesty! May my tongue singe if it utters something ill-omened. Pooranji has abandoned the palace for some destination unknown. We searched for him since morning until sunset, without finding a trace of him. We found this note in his Golden Palace, the content of which I cannot understand."

(Salwan takes the note from the attendant. The attendant leaves. Loona request Salwan to read the note. Salwan reads it aloud.)

"Mother! I depart, leaving your palace, your shade, your village. Going far away where there is a light of truth, where there is no Earth or Sky, no day or night. Far-off, where there are no walls of kinship between people, only one colour and no other, only one path and no other. Afar I go where no door is closed, unbound without limits. I am going to the place, which is beyond words and attributes, which is hue-less, beyond birth and death, infinite, neither alight nor dark. I depart to a place where religion is action, knowledge and virtue. I move on breaking all bonds of illusion, breaking the cord of false shame, burning the jungle of darkness. I move away from gulping the oceans of hatred, breaking away from phony customs. Loona, I move contented but with sorrow to have caused contempt to your craving flesh, for which Pooran is innocent. Pooran rose above lust, which is a momentary, fevering tide in blood, for which he has no guilt. It is just a game played by destiny.

So Loona! I go with my last salutation to you in this birth. Adieu! Adieu! Adieu!"

(Salwan turns silent for some time after reading the note. He laughs hysterically and then cries. He calls Pooran's name aloud.)

"Pooran, O Pooran! Please come back! Do not leave this world for the sake of your mother. I swear, for the sake of your father, please return back. Where is the loyalty in a woman? For this shameless, wicked woman please do not lay your life. A woman is a white lie, a crook, smell of a poisonous flower. Loona of the ilk, a low-born untouchable seeking sensuous favours from her son is a curse to the womb that gave birth to her. I swear on your seething words, that I shall keep burning until I quench my hands in vile black blood of Loona."

Loona concealing her nervousness speaks impulsively, "Yes! Yes! Loona is wicked because she is a woman. Her pedigree and blood are wicked because she is a helpless woman. A while ago, she was the holy Ganges water, now she is a lowborn. Just now, she was a bud of Jasmine, but now she has become a thorn. A while ago she was light, now is all darkness. A man's love is like a honeybee, honey on the tongue and poison on the sting. Loona is guiltless, yet she is prepared to die. But your Majesty, Loona also has the right to say something. Loona is not characterless; she is a virtuous, loving wife. It is Pooran, who has sinned. No wonder, blaming a woman is a tradition in all ages. Reproving women is the basis of all religions. Condemning women is assumed to always be right. Spitting on her face and terming her a lowly creature is, perhaps deeply imbibed, in the culture of man. I remained mum, for the fear that people would reject me as a yelling stepmother who is passing blame for her own selfish ends like Kaikeyee[14]. But, I have to call a spade a spade. He insisted that you have no right to be called a mother, you are a beloved. He crooned that I am young and of his age. You are a bijou of my soul, he'd said. He called me his charming rose, his intoxicating wine and a dream in reality."

Salwan icily, "It is sheer infidelity, a nonsense lie."

"I am still half way, your Majesty! Just see this scar on my delicate wrist; it is a gift of the beast that resides in Pooran. Have you ever heard a son holding a mother's wrist saying, 'O the beautiful! O moonfaced, your beauty simmers in my dreams. From your lips spills my cup of wine. Your scented beautiful locks bite me like a black snake. Without you, my bed looks deserted.' If a mother tries to free herself, he gives a devilish laugh and throws her in the bed. Your Majesty! Had I not put the fear of your ire in his mind, I couldn't have saved my honour."

"Stop it Loona! No more narration of the blazing saga in your parching words. Do not pour more molten lead into my ears. My blood boils and the heart scalds with every searing word of yours. If truth resides in this story then it is my blood that is a culprit and not Loona. My blood is polluted, debauch, and stinks of wickedness," Salwan in a bewildered tone, "Loona! Sitting in front of you, I swear, I will drink my own blood. I will stitch my wounds with my own blood, wash the blemish of my blood with my own blood. I will cut Pooran into pieces. Loona! Once I find even his dead body, I will break its legs, remove its eyeballs and feed it to the vultures and dogs."

(Salwan moves out deeply hurt, leaving Loona alone. Ira enters.)

Ira is dazed, "Loona! What is all this I hear? Blatant lies. This is sin. This is disastrous."

"Yes, it is a lie. Yes, it is a terrible sin. To get salvation from one sin, one has to resort to another sin. Sin is annihilated when it exceeds a limit. For Loona, there is no distinction between sin and virtue; there is no difference between day and night. It is the gory history of abuse of women and their endless insult, which to me is the biggest sin. The kindness of a woman is the highest blessing and her exasperation is a curse. How do the sin and virtue differ? They are two sides of the same coin, mutually interchangeable. They are measured with the yardstick of creeds laid by religions for their convenience. Religion is a body that, itself, is in a deep slumber", Loona continues with a stiff face, "The real sin is not to know oneself, but not understanding one's own light and dark side. Without right and without consent, mating of bodies without a match is a sin. Using Loona's virgin body, the way Salwan does is a sin."

Ira still not coming to the terms, "Loona! Are you in your senses? Every word of yours is a psychotic outburst. Every utterance of yours is inebriated. Pooran was always innocent and guiltless. He is like a baby bird in the nest, is pure…"

Loona interrupts, "Ira, yes I am very much in my senses. Yes, he is pure and innocent like a baby bird in a nest. Pooran is my light and my flame. But, a woman is the pot of nectar over the hood of a snake. If someone drinks it, becomes immortal and if one rejects it gets death. It is said that an Ashoka tree doesn't blossom until a virgin kicks its root. This is neither an insult nor hostility against the tree, but a favour to it by the virgin. I was pained to see Pooran, a blossomless Ashoka tree. I kicked his roots. I injected sinful poison into his chastity, with an aim that the blemish would prompt him to grow and flower that would sustain him on Earth for generations to come. Whenever people would congregate and talk, they would fondly narrate the story of Pooran's poise. They would curse Loona and adore Pooran. Perhaps this would save young daughters like Loona from coercive marriage to Salwan and sons like Pooran will not be wounded by a bruised heart."

(Loona laughs loudly and then starts crying.)

~

The Lamenting First Lady

(King Chaudhal in his palace is talking to his daughter Ichcharan.)

"O folks! Daughters' grief is unfathomable. They say daughters are like butterflies. They are agile gazelles, a short-lived delight of their fathers' place, who go away. Listen O folks, a distressed daughter's aggrieved father makes a submission, never beget a daughter."

Ichcharan laments, "Yes dear father, you rightly said, not to beget daughters. Giving birth to a daughter would lower your stature; it will take away the fragrance from the embroidered flowers on your white turban. Their birth shrinks the resources of the house. They are the termites, once they make an entry into a house, they don't spare its doors, its walls and its roof."

"Dear daughter! Daughters are the treasures of the house. They have no one alike. They increase the fortune, the honour and the status of the family. But my daughter, your father fails to understand how life took such tragic turn for you? Having son, husband and father, today there is no one whom you can call yours. How can this helpless father share your grief? The Earth does not give me a moment of respite and the sky doesn't provide me support. If I decide to send you back, my heart won't permit and if you stay in your father's house there is a loss of face. I am puzzled with this dilemma."

Ichcharan pleads, "Listen my virtuous father, please do not deport me to that house again. The snakes of gloom sting me there; the mere thought of it poisons my blood. May your daughter die without a shroud, her bones go uncared, without being gathered.

A daughter begs for her shroud from you. It's better to die here than to rot there."

"My little princess! Do not utter such evil words. They sink my heart. O daughter! I understand your anguish but have no cure for it. If I find a medicine for your pain, I'm ready to pay any sum for it."

"O dear father, no healer can prescribe a cure for a daughter's agony. Her pain ends only when they are burned over a pyre. It is a disease that has penetrated into the bones of the society that they have to spit blood from the instant of their birth to the moment of their death."

"My dear daughter, they say that a daughter's life is like a sandal tree that drinks poison yet spreads fragrance. She absorbs the sting of the cruel destiny quietly," tries to pacify Chaudhal.

Ichcharan's words remain gloomy, "Dear father, daughters sadly are not worth a sandal tree. People sometimes, to pamper, equate them to the tree. Daughters, in fact, are the timbers of bitter trees. They are sold effortlessly, as no woodworm comes near them for bitterness, and no termite eats them either. Daughters being bitter wood, their bones are suited for sawing to make wooden beams to raise high palaces. Daughters are the bevy of birds on the contours of time who fly carrying the lost age in their beaks into the future. They carry the visage of the bygone era through their wombs into the future, perishing themselves in the process. It is the daughter, who echo the tragedy in every era recreating through it the pain in her womb. She is a protagonist of the past, the present and the future, an endless saga of pain."

"Daughter dear, no daughter stays with her parents forever. Her stay with them is limited to her playful childhood days.

Adolescence arrives and her mother spins for her dowry and her father sweats for her match. As she attains maturity, the daughter becomes a mother one day. My coolest shade, I do not know how do I alleviate your sorrow. What a horrid husband I chose for you, I deeply regret. I do not find a place to drown or hide myself."

"My virtuous father, a daughters' grief is abysmal; it is deeper than the oceans, heavier than the mountains. If daughters turn out to be base, they bring shame. If they are unpleasant, no one agrees to marry them. If they are beautiful, people caution you for them. If they become a widow, they bear the guilt for it. If she remains single, you remain worried until your death. Some people kill them at birth. Their birth shakes the walls of the house and a family's esteem is lowered."

(A maid makes entry.)

"Your Majesty! Your Majesty! A horseman on a flying horse just arrived at the palace gate. He gave a disturbing message and turned back."

Chaudhal asks, "Who was he? What message did he leave? Tell me quickly."

Maid replies, "Your Majesty! Despite my repeated insistence, the horseman did not disclose. He just informed Ichcharan to come to Kot Sial at least once. Otherwise, the King will kill her son Pooran."

Ichcharan is stunned, "What did you utter? The King will kill Pooran? For which fault of his, is the father going to slaughter his son?"

"O Royal Daughter! How would I, the lesser being, know? He said to tell Ichcharan to come if she wants to see her son's face for the last time."

Ichcharan with a deep sigh, "Alas! I have not seen my dear Pooran's face even once to this day. Do not put the dagger of these words in my heart."

Maid hesitantly, "Reverend Royal Madam, the messenger said that Prince Pooran longed for beloved's love from his mother Loona. He forced upon her for an adulterous liaison. The news is that Pooran escaped to the forest abandoning the palace. The King's soldiers, however, hunted and captured him. The King has issued the order to severe his limbs."

(Ichcharan collapses with the trauma. King Chaudhal and maid rush towards her.)

~

The Royal Diktat

(A big crowd has congregated in an open arena. On one side of the arena is King Salwan, seated with Loona and his courtiers. Pooran is standing in the center of the crowd. The executioners are standing behind Pooran with naked swords. Pooran's feet are shackled. A weird clamour engulfs the crowd. Ripping through the crowd holding her emotions Ichcharan moves towards Pooran.)

Ichcharan asks, "Pooran! Is it correct that my Pooran is less than perfect?"

"Yes dear mother, your Pooran is less than perfect. Here perfection is a privilege of only the mighty. Here there is no truth, but only all-pervading lies. Here one who claims to have an identity has no face. Here those who have their limbs intact behave as lames. Here everyone lives bereft of conscience."

"Is it true that my Pooran has sinned? Is my milk, he was fed with, so mean?" asks Ichcharan again in disbelief.

"Dear mother, there is no fault with your milk. A mother's milk can never be fallible. Motherhood is a temple, but without a flame. Its alleys are dark, inhabited by bats. A few birds reside here in their own interest and fly away for food at dawn, returning by the sunset. They noisily chirp, tweet and quarrel before settling in their nests for the night. Due to their ignorance, their fledglings fall from the nest, die and are consumed by moths. I too am a featherless baby bird who has fallen from the nest to die an early death, carried by an army of ants to their burrow. Lying in the burrow it rots and spreads foul smell."

Ichcharan cries helplessly, "Pooran, your mother is unable to bear your words. They scorch her heart. My dear son, today the affection of my milk is put to shame. Your own mother is cursing your mother's womb, for the stigma she has earned, perhaps for some sins committed in previous births. Why did you chose to commit such a sinful act just for the fair skin of lowborn cobbler's daughter? There are scores of damsels around, more beautiful than Loona. Had you once passed a hint, I would have gotten you any of them for marriage. I feel that I were better childless than having a child who is a blot on our entire clan."

"Listen dear mother, here every shadow of mother's milk betrays her. Here everyone earns sin taking undue advantage from someone known or unknown. Here everyone wants to consume the wine from the flesh, and beauty of another. Here everyone's pleasure-seeking conscience never allows the mind to come to rest. Here all are embodied as Cupids blindfolded, stringing their bows with honeybees, arrows adorned with flowers and leaves. All are offspring of weaknesses."

Ichcharan pleads with tears, "Pooran! Before this matter comes to finality, before your body is maimed and burnt, I want Pooran to decline from this sin. This will save the honour of my milk and my womb from shame."

Pooran replies calmly, "Dear mother, everyone is condemned to be born on this Earth to live with humiliation. Everyone falls here in one's own eyes and is unable to face one's own conscience. Those who live here are dead even before their birth and exist hauling their corpse on their shoulders. Here clay consumes clay, it is the clay that marries other clay, and another clay is born. After passing through eighty-four lakh cycles of births and deaths, clay assumes a human name and earns its sins. Clay is unable to discriminate the purpose of its birth, the myth remains covered under folds of mystery. It is for good that my clay gets freed of this birth, in this way for which I am not ashamed. Pooran symbolizes all life dear mother, Salwan a father and a guardian who is unable to understand him. Ichcharan represents the mother of all life who suffers pain to sustain the life. Loona is a distraction from the path, an obstruction that devours life. She is a stumbling block, a stone on the way that everyone hits consciously or unconsciously sapping life from life. Life turns unintelligible, an unlivable burden merely counting days, abhorring oneself, detesting anyone's company. I desire to put an end to it. So that no Salwan hereafter marries a young daughter and no daughter has to helplessly return to her sires, lowering their honour. No Loona ever ruins her youth begging love from an alien. No more trading of flesh. Hereafter no father maims his son and no son is dismembered. No Pooran escapes from life loathing himself. I aspire, every man and every woman to live with profound dignity. I desire Pooran to perish and emerge as a symbol, a lodestar, a saga that guides everyone from straying from the path."

(Salwan and Loona move towards Pooran and Ichcharan.)

Salwan thunders, "Ichcharan, what a dreadful sin you have committed! You gave birth to a son who disgraced the pain of your womb….And what sin did I commit, to face such atrocious destiny, that coerces me to kill my own son? Today onwards, all my days will be darkened and the rest of my life will be spent with shame. Rest of my breaths won't have fortitude to keep my head high. Today my own shadow hangs its head in ignominy in front of me. O my Lord, what kind of sun you have rendered me today, so dull and so colourless. It looks as if an eighth colour has been mingled with my sunshine, eclipsing my radiance entirely.

This colour has fetched all gloom, muffled silence, obliterating the colours of all directions. Today I am ashamed of myself, I am ashamed of Ichcharan, I stand small before Loona, I feel to have betrayed my people. O God, I feel I am dead, yet I breathe. I wish I were dead."

(Salwan points towards Pooran.)

"O the offspring of my dirty blood running through my blue veins, the shadow of Ichcharan's foul breath, born at an inauspicious hour to bring this dark era, you lowered my prestige, brought a blot on my clan. You are my cursed creation, of an evil moment. I doubt that you are my own blood; I can't find my radiance in you. I don't see the culture and the belief of this era in you. Are you from the Stone Age that you couldn't see the sin in your mother's body? You rejected your relation of milk with her, by your inappropriate advances."

Pooran with serene demeanour, "Here, every age is the Stone Age treating its culture as its maid. Man has always been boorish and will continue be so. Corporeal worship is the religion in every age. The golden deer always beguiles the *Panchvati*[22] that finds pleasure in all that is material. Every age watches Shrupnakha's[28]nose severed. This is an age when Pooran stands accused, an age will come that will indict Salwan. Here sin will remain, only sin will sustain. The alleys of human heart have always been dark and will remain murky. The dark sun will continue to rise every day."

Salwan roars, "What do you intend to say? That you are absolutely blameless?"

"Here no one is blameless, nor is anyone blameworthy. It is the compulsion from four directions that fetches the blame."

Salwan loudly, "O son of a limmer, what was the compulsion that forced you to see the ugliness in your mother's milk? Why haven't your hands, that touched your mother, been infected by leprosy?"

Pooran replies, "No son will be able to answer such question. This is the compulsion, when the answer has to struggle for words. Short of words the truth becomes blameworthy."

"Then the unspoken truth is that you were dissolute with your mother."

Pooran stays calm and says, "Yes! It is an unspoken truth that I touched my mother with my dirty hands and sinned against mother's milk."

(Salwan gives a slap on Pooran's face and rumbles in fury.)

"Take away…! Take away this unspoken black truth! Make him wear the dress of blood soaked words. Take him away, cut him into pieces, feed his flesh to vultures, and throw his bones to dogs. Throw his limbless body into the barren well."

Loona also pleads, "Your Majesty, be merciful. He is a brainless adolescent. Don't be so cruel with him."

Salwan shudders, "Get out of my way. Do not touch me."

Crowd yells, "Be pitiful with him."

Ichcharan cries with her face soaked in tears, "My son is blameless. Do not accuse him like this."

Salwan sizzles, "It is an order, keep quiet! Remove the mother of this blemished son away from my sight. Throw some dirt on her head and some on mine. Every mother babbles like Ichcharan to cover her son's flaws, even if it is his improper advances towards the mother. She would always advocate for him to be of high character…Executioners come closer, raise your swords and severe the hands of this lecherous creature. Take away life from his feet, which rose on the mother's bed and soiled the sacred relation between mother and son…..And the hands flaming hatred, spitting poison like a five-tongued snake. Kill the hooded snake that has stung my family. Remove its venom and show it to the world."

Ichcharan pleads, "I beg for your pity. Please don't kill this mute child. I am ready to lay my life in place of Pooran. He is not the one who has sinned, I am the sinner. Uproot and cut the mother of the sin. Pronounce the punishment for my sin."

Loona again entreats, "Yes Royal Highness have some pity on him."

Salwan bitterly, "I am unable to understand anything. Do not try to make me understand now. Do not come close to me. Do not put more words into this flaming saga. Please, end this burning tale. No more torture to me, executioners raise your swords, slay the sin and earn virtue."

(Executioners severe hands and feet of Pooran. Ichcharan becomes unconscious and falls. Salwan turns his back on the writhing maimed body of Pooran. Loud wailing and lamentation fills the arena. An intense storm crosses ripping the arena. Loona sits by the side of squirming body of Pooran covering her face with hands and crying.)

Epilogue-I

Forbidden fruits allure. And a lusty woman ever remains an object of attraction. Loona is one such piece of figment. Loona, the central character, in the legendary tale of Pooran Bhagat comes to us through Punjabi folk songs, through oral tradition and through bedtime stories since ages. The legend is played on stage and depicted in the form of street plays in front of masses in villages, towns, and cities of undivided Punjab and Himachal Pradesh. There is probably no native of Punjab and Himachal who has not heard the story of Pooran Bhagat. During the reign of Maharaja Ranjit Singh, prominent *kissakaar*[17], Qaadar Yaar scripted it for a first time in a *kissa*[16] form. Qaadar Yaar (1805-92) was a foremost Punjabi poet of 19th century. A Sandhu *jaat*[11] by caste, he was born in the village Machihe of Shekhupura district (now in Pakistan) in 1805, largely known among common folks through his Kissa Pooran Bhagat. It was a time when Maharaja Ranjit Singh ruled Punjab and Hari Singh Nalwa was the commander-in-chief of his army. He was a benign ruler, who cared for all his subjects. Though himself unlettered, he patronised men of letters and artists in his court. Pleased with his Kissa Pooran Bhagat, Qaadar Yaar was rewarded with a piece of land and a well by the Maharaja. Qaadar Yaar enjoyed the patronage of both Lahore *darbaar*, and Sikh *sardaars*[25], in West and East parts of Punjab. Qaadar Yaar narrated the popular version of the story. His poetry is in Gurumukhi[9] and Shahmukhi[27]. Traditionally, the story of Pooran Bhagat has many versions with minor and major variations. Qaadar Yaar himself created two adaptations 'Pooran Bhagat' and 'Vaar Pooran Bhagat'. His two accounts are not the same.

In Qaadar Yaar's portrayal Loona is a low-caste beautiful young maiden from Chamba. She's brought to Sialkot by King Salwan as his second wife. Salwan is of Loona's father's age, but age didn't count for the rich and mighty. Salwan had a son from his first wife, Ichcharan. King Salwan and Queen Ichcharan were a child-less couple long before Pooran was born to Ichcharan after many religious rituals, propitiation of planets and Gods. His birth naturally brought immense joy to the King and his kingdom. But destiny had something else in store. Astrologers cast the birth chart of the infant prince. Reading through his stars fortunetellers prognosticated that the child's stars were such that he was to be kept away from public eye and also away from the eyes of his parents till he turns twelve. Soothsayers warned that any dilution in what had been prescribed might bring misfortune to the King, Queen and their kingdom. Going by the warning of clairvoyance Pooran was kept in isolation under royal care for twelve long years.

Just as the period of isolation ended Pooran went to his mother Ichcharan, who became too emotional to see her enchanting grown up son. As she hugged him with deep maternal affection, the joy of meeting the son after a long time flowed from her eyes. Thereafter, Pooran mooved to meet his stepmother Loona.

It was during this period of seclusion when Loona was brought to Sialkot by the King as his second wife. Young Loona found no attraction in King Salwan, for the huge age-gap between the two. As Pooran entered in Loona's chamber, Loona had the first sight of charming, young Pooran. His innocent smile, captivating disposition mesmerized Loona. Loona saw in him a man of her age. After the first meeting, her eyes followed Pooran. She craved for his society. Her desire to be intimate with him got louder with every passing day. Loona made advances towards him. And one day, she revealed her attraction towards Pooran as woman and man. Pooran got deeply shaken with her amorous advances. Discovering that she had lost her capacity to discriminate between right and wrong, he exhorts that she being his father's wife and is naturally his mother. Loona isn't convinced; the fire of illegitimate passion blurred her vision. She relentlessly persuaded him. Pooran, however, remained firm in his position. He advocated social norms and said that though she did not carry him in her womb, did not give birth to him, did not suckle him yet, being his father's wife, she was naturally his mother. Finding no effect of her illicit entreaties on the young lad, deeply hurt Loona turned furious. Rejection gave her a feeling of being disparaged. She contemplated revenge.

Loona knew that the King in his obsession for her would remain on her side, in her right and also in her wrong. She approached him and made an emotional appeal, 'Pooran has a tainted eye on me. He has made unethical advances towards me and tried to outrage me. He is as much my son as yours. But such lowly act by son of King Salwan…'

Salwan blinded by the glare of his newly acquired wife believed her words and summoned his son Pooran. Without a fair trial, he ordered to have his limbs dismembered and thrown into the well. Pooran, however, didn't die and stayed alive eating herbs in the well. Later Guru Gorakh Nath[8], who happensed to pass by, found mutilated Pooran in the well. Guru, with his magical powers, brought his severed body together and christened him as Pooran Bhagat, the name that stands for a complete devotee.

In Qaadar Yaar's kissa, Pooran is the central figure, Ichchaharan is a silent and marginalized woman whereas Loona is a low-caste promiscuous woman who is responsible for Pooran's woes. The story moves in a medieval mindset when people largely believed supernatural. Salwan, though acts foolhardily, first marrying a girl of age to be his daughter and then severely punishing his innocent son, is not considered wrong because he's a male and a King and no one could question him. There is no sympathy for Loona in *kissa* as social order of those times considered her culpable for being a woman and a lowborn.

Metaphysically, Pooran represents Punjab of the 18th century. *Kissakaar* through Pooran's story is attempting to bring the status of Punjab during those times. Punjab, which was running in bad days with invasion of Ahmed Shah Abdali, misrule of smalltime rulers. It was much severed into parts, mutilated, and low in his spirit much like Pooran. Under the fine stewardship of Maharaja Ranjit Singh, Punjab becomes united and gains its glory. Though the story of Qaadar Yaar succeeds in that part, yet the neglect of Ichcharan and depicting Loona as villain, both victims of circumstances, cannot be accepted as such. Qaadar Yaar, however, fulfils his duty towards his patron through his poetic excellence.

Twentieth century poet and writer Shiv Kumar Batalvi, however looks at *kissa* from an entirely different perspective in his timeless epic Loona. Shiv, through his opus, brings out physical and beyond physical the psychic dimension of Loona's agitations, her churnings and her deep cravings. The melodrama also reveals the suffering of Pooran, who is the victim of circumstances. My narrative in this work has largely followed Shiv's creation.

Qaadar Yaar's thinking, to an extent, was subordinate to his patron. His ballad toes the line of folkways existing at that time. Qaadar Yaar's portrayal verse-play is Pooran-centric whereas Shiv Batalvi's made it Loona-centric. Shiv was a progressive writer and his tone is rebellious. It was the post-colonial period when he recreated his verse-drama. India was liberated, so was its air. Shiv attained adulthood from boyhood breathing liberated air, so is his poetry. Shiv's poetic sensibilities ventilated the anguish of Loona who is a woman, and a low-caste untouchable, coming from lower strata of society. The dissenting woman in Loona wonders as to how her alluring beauty has become a curse, a bondage, rather than being an asset. She is pushed out of her homeland with a man of her father's age. This is a deep wound to a budding young woman. Batalvi's approach is, however, not didactic conforming to the moral teaching. To develop the story from Loona's perspective, Batalvi made certain departures from the traditional version. He ends the story with Pooran's limbs severed from his body. This is to make it appeal more logical to a rational mind. Freedom, and equality, are the centre-points of his story. The equality of caste, class, sexes, which Batalvi has amply asserted. Shiv has transformed it to Loona's story from Pooran's tale.

Shiv dared to underscore the inner fire in a woman in the society where female interest in sexuality is deplored, and is considered lust. He brought her expression of sexuality into a formal sphere. Batalvi touches the core of the woman who is deeply bruised after being treated as a commodity, and is married off to a man thrice her age. Loona is questioning old conventions, but she has no courage against Salwan. She rather behaves in an irresponsible manner towards Pooran. Shiv's plot ends with death of Pooran, but he not being a hero, doesn't create too much tragic emotions. The narrative is able to convey the message loudly where Loona remains a protagonist.

End Notes-I

1. *Ahiravan*: The demon king of netherworld in Hindu mythology.

2. *Apooran*: Incomplete

3. *Chakor*: Sanskrit name of partridge bird that symbolizes intense love. The bird is believed to be in love with the Moon and it gazes the Moon constantly.

4. Chamba: Situated on the banks of river Ravi, Chamba is a town in Chamba district in the state of Himachal Pradesh in India.

5. *Chatak*: A member of cuckoo order of birds. Used in the ancient Indian literature, mythology and poetry as a metaphor for deep yearning. The mythical bird is said to keep its beak up in the sky and awaiting the first raindrop to quench its thirst.

6. Cycles of birth and death: According to Hindu belief every soul goes through eighty-four lakh cycles of birth and death in different forms namely birds, animals, trees etc. till one gets human form. In human form the journey of the soul starts towards God.

7. Ganges: The holy river of Hindus.

8. Guru Gorakh Nath: A Hindu yogi saint, one of the nine saints also known as *Navnath*. Temples dedicated to him are in many parts of India, particularly in eponymous city of Gorakhpur in province of Uttar Pradesh. Legends say that he travelled widely across Indian subcontinent during his lifetime.

9. Gurumukhi: Most common script used for writing in Punjabi language written from left to right, adopted in Indian province of Punjab.

10. *Indra*: Ancient Vedic deity of Hinduism. The king of gods, the god of seasons, a great warrior who conquers anti-gods. He is believed to bring rains as the god of thunderbolts.

11. *Jaat*: Traditionally an agriculture based community largely in rural parts of Northern India, that is, Punjab, Haryana, Western Uttar Pradesh, Delhi, Rajasthan.

12. Jaggery: Concentrated product of cane juice and often date or palm sap consumed in Asia.

13. *Kamadev*: Hindu god of human longing, desire and love.

14. Kaikeyee: The second consort of King Dasratha and the Queen of Ayodhya. She was the mother of Prince Bharata, the younger brother of Lord Rama.

15. King Dasratha: Maharaja of ancient kingdom of Koshala with its capital Ayodhya. Father of Lord Rama.

16. *Kissa*: Story

17. *Kissakaar*: Storyteller

18. Kot Sial: Fort Sial

19. *Mahayagna*: Ritual of grand sacrifice to the sacred fire with chanting of mantras.

20. *Malhar*: Hindustani classical raga associated with torrential rains. According to legend, *Malhar* when sung correctly by a highly accomplished singer, it could induce rainfall.

21. *Narsimha Avatar*: A fierce incarnation of the Hindu god Vishnu, in the form of part lion and part man. Lord *Narsimha*

killed the demon king *Hirnakashyap* to save his righteous son *Prahalad's* life from his father.

22. *Panchvati*: Forest home of Lord Rama at Nashik (Maharashtra) where he resided with his wife Sita and younger brother Lakshmana during crucial phase of his exile from Ayodhya. There are five (*pancham*) Banyan trees here and hence area is called *Panchvati*. As per the legend Sita saw a beautiful golden deer and asked Rama to get it for her. While Rama went away in chase of the deer, Sita was abducted by demon King Ravana of Lanka. In battle that ensued between forces of Rama and Ravana, the demon king was killed by Lord Rama.

23. *Pooran*: Complete

24. *Rati*: Hindu goddess of love, carnal desire and sexual pleasure. Rati is the female counterpart of *Kamadeva*, the god of love.

25. *Sardaar*: Commander; little nobility.

26. Sarma: Rig Veda describes it as the bitch of Indra. The divine bitch considered as the mother of all dogs.

27. Shahmukhi: Parso-Arabic alphabets used for Punjabi language, written from right to left largely adopted in province of Punjab in Pakistan.

28. Shrupnakha: Sister of demon King Ravana of Sri Lanka who was smitten by Rama's good looks tried to entice Rama. Rejected by Rama who was faithful to his wife Sita, Shrupnakha was infuriated. Lakshmana, the younger brother of Rama punished her by cutting off her nose.

29. Sialkot: A city now in the state of Punjab, Pakistan.

30. Swati: Star with English name Arcturus. As per Vedic Astrology the first drops of rain fall on the Earth during rainy season in the northern hemisphere as Moon is seen at Swati star. The first drops of rain are therefore termed as *Swati*.

31. Udhay City: The native city of Salwan's wife Ichcharan.

TISHYARAKSHITA

Characters-II

ASHOKA : Third Emperor of Maurya Dynasty (322 BCE -185 BCE)

BINDUSARA : Ashoka's father

SUSHIMA : Eldest son of Bindusara

VITASHOKA : Womb younger brother of Ashoka

ASANDHIMITRA : Chief Queen of Ashoka

DEVI : First queen of Ashoka

KARUVAKI : Ashoka's queen from Kalinga region

PADMAVATI : Crown Prince Kunala's mother

TISHYARAKSHITA : Youngest queen of Ashoka

KUNALA : Crown Prince, son of Ashoka

RADHAGUPTA : Prime Minister of Ashoka

KHALLATAKA : Second Minister of Asoka

SAKULA : Attendant of Tishyarakshita

The Third Maurya

Succession to a position of power is rarely easy. It is often guided by intrigue, and sometimes by bloodshed. Ashoka's accession to the throne of Magadh also had its fair share of scheming and ample bloodshed. For his ungainly looks, craggy appearance and turbulent temperament as a youth, Ashoka was not the first preference of his father Maharaja Bindusara Amitrochates[2]. Good-looking Sushima, the eldest half-brother of Ashoka, was the favoured child of Bindusara and naturally his choice for succession. Bindusara ruled for more than a quarter of the century, over a vast empire inherited from his father Chandragupta Maurya. His domain extended from Hindu Kush in the west, beyond Bengal in the east and from the Himalayas in the north, to a part of Tamil land in the south.

During his reign, Bindusara acquired sixteen queens of different pedigrees and had a hundred sons with them. Ashoka was, obviously, destined for the task of removing them from his path to the safety of his throne. The grind of securing himself and his formal coronation took four years after the death of his father. Ashoka was clever, resolute, less tempted towards trifling pleasures. He abhorred the caste system and ostentatious rituals by haughty Brahmins[8] who created an unwarranted fear of Gods in the minds of people. He was not an easy choice of women who preferred external appearance combined with riches and power. Being brave and astute when compared to his other siblings, Bindusara used him for various campaigns in his empire, on his council's advice. Sushima, the eldest son of the King had a boyish streak in him. Though charming and dignified, he enjoyed the company of princesses, courtesans and friends. Sushima respected the Vedas and ritualistic Brahmins, who loved him in equal measure. Brahmins preferred the propagation of a rigid cast system with their superiority over other castes. High priests felt their clique would be in safe hands under Sushima, as compared to Ashoka, who was mentally tough, brave, egalitarian and quick to take decisions. Ashoka's superior skills in weaponry, ability to take decisions with lesser dependence on advisers made him a preferred choice to command the troops among majority of King's ministers.

When it came to make the choice between his two princes to lead the Taxila[32]campaign, Bindusara wavered. His heart was with his favourite Prince Sushima, whereas his mind was inclined towards Ashoka. Ultimately, with promptings of his ministers, his head took lead over his heart and Ashoka was directed to move to Taxila to oversee the uprising in the Western Province of Punjab[23]. But this was not without a lurking fear in the heart of Maharaja that a successful Ashoka might become a threat to the King's own authority. Bindusara's mind was never away from the fact of history that, two centuries ago in Rajgriha[25], Ajatshatru succeeded his father Maharaja Bimbisar by imprisoning and then killing him, who in turn was later killed by his son Udayin in a further war of succession. Ashoka, however had no such design in his mind against Maharaja but he hated Sushima for being a likely choice for succession. In fact, the hatred between the two princes was mutual. Ashoka's source of hate lay somewhere in Sushima's unworthiness to lead Aryavarta[6]in eyes of Ashoka and also an attempt that was made on Ashoka's life at the behest of Sushima. Sushima reviled Ashoka as he knew that Ashoka was made of superior material, he was hardened and could stake the claim over the throne of Magadh, on the basis of merit.

Ashoka's camp was jubilant with the King's decision choosing him for the Taxila campaign, but it was received with heart-burn by Sushima and his mother Gopali, and with deep indignation by the Brahmins, who had considerable influence in the court. Brahmins knew that if Ashoka returned successful from his Taxila mission he would be closer to the throne of the Empire.

Ashoka began to make the preparations for his move to Taxila. He appointed a small force consisting of war elephants, excellent horsemen and a few hundred selected foot soldiers. The commanders chosen by him to lead the divisions were personally known to him. The troop strength was kept deliberately small by the Prince, to facilitate faster movement. His belief rested upon quality over quantity. Ashoka, with his slender column, left with a warm send off by people, ministers, officers and Maharaja. Priests had at least one reason to be happy, as they believed that with such a small force at his disposal Ashoka was destined to taste defeat at Taxila.

The distance between Pataliputra[19]and the city of Taxila was close to two thousand kilometers. The journey through forests, villages, suburbs, cities and across rivers on the way was arduous. But, against Ashoka's indomitable spirit no task was insurmountable.

Moving swiftly, camping and rejuvenating overnight at locations close to river streams, the army reached its destination in thirty days. The prince was clear that reaching early had its own advantages, which would catch the adversary off-guard and give them less time for preparedness.

On his way to his destination, Ashoka did his homework well by talking to the farmers, merchants and traders to get to the bottom of the actual cause of displeasure in the minds of Taxilans that led to the uprising. He gathered that their displeasure was not against Maharaja but against the officers of the Crown. The officials sent from Pataliputra to collect the legitimate taxes, on behalf of Maharaja, did their job diligently for many years. However, for the past few years corruption had slowly crept in the cadres and majority of officials did not restrain themselves from seeking a bigger amount, not for the kingdom but for filling their own coffers. Many businessmen left the city, unable to bear the exploitation. There was a general feeling that Pataliputra, far away from Punjab, has less affinity towards their province compared to the Central Province. Moreover, people of Punjab historically had never submitted to the culture propagated by Brahmins and as such needed a different kind of treatment. Ashoka had capacity to see a big picture without losing sight on finer details. He understood that all these issues needed to be settled, for establishing long-term peace in the area.

The stories about Ashoka's prowess and legends woven around his bravery had already reached the ears of Taxilans before Ashoka actually put his foot on its soil. A group of ministers of Taxila, loyal to Maharaja tried to convince the local Commander of uprising to have a dialogue with the Prince to iron out the differences. But the Commander was not prepared to listen. When the Prince and the Commander came face to face, seeing a small body of army with Ashoka, the Commander in his over confidence suddenly ordered his troops to attack. The skirmish had just begun, Ashoka leading from the front aimed his arrow at the Commander and killed him in his one infallible shot. Consequently, his troops, who were halfheartedly engaged in fight, came to their knees and surrendered. Ashoka and his commanders were pleased as the battle was won without much bloodshed.

In the meeting that ensued between the ministers and high officers of Taxila with Ashoka, Prince got their faith pledged in Maharaja was once again. Ashoka renewed the oath of obedience with them, to the laws of the Great Indian Empire[33]. He ordered the return of money to businessmen, which was unlawfully extracted and instructed to call back the traders who left the city due to the oppression by the King's officers. He instilled faith among the citizens, and established the confidence that the province of Punjab was as dear to Mauryas as any other. Populace was overwhelmed with Ashoka's prompt action with fairness and firmness. Ashoka was a much-relieved man. He was conducted by the ministers through the streets of the lovely city of Taxila with people having lined up on both sides, showering beautiful flowers and overwhelming cheers. Ministers and high officers of Taxila requested the Imperial Commander to get a permanent Viceroy appointed at Taxila for sustainable peace. They had Prince Ashoka in their minds suitable for the job, as they wished him to remain with them. Ashoka liked the proposal, but the proposition required King's approval.

The King at Pataliputra received regular reports on the developments at Taxila through his spies and through couriers dispatched by the Prince. King had all the reasons to be happy that his choice of army commander for Taxila mission proved to be correct. But the Brahmins and the priestly lobby at Pataliputra did not remain mute spectators to Ashoka's successful mission. They had undeservedly enjoyed huge privileges from the state for many years, which they could not afford to let go so easily. They fabricated stories against the Prince for Maharaja highlighting his higher ambitions and about his raising a formidable force at Taxila that would be a threat to the Maharaja in times to come. King vacillated for some time but finally decided to recall Ashoka from Taxila. But the Emperor did not know what he would do with the Prince at Pataliputra. Ashoka, the man brimming with energy, could not be made to sit idle and was required to be given a suitable assignment. Moreover, the two Princes sitting close at Pataliputra would again be at each other's neck. After prolonged deliberations, the emperor's council advised him to make Ashoka the Viceroy of Ujjain, and Sushima the Viceroy of Taxila. The Emperor nodded.

Ashoka was summoned back form Taxila. Prince wasn't too happy about this abrupt development but this was King's command. Much to the dismay of Taxilans, Ashoka and his army made a move to Pataliputra. Before leaving Taxila, he warned the administration not to venture against Pataliputra taking the law into their hands in future but to address their grievances, if any, with the King. Ashoka was back to Pataliputra, as swiftly as he had travelled to Taxila a few months ago.

~

 On his arrival at Pataliputra, Ashoka first reported to the King and deeply bowed before him. King embraced him showing warmth.

"As you are aware, dear father, I could accomplish the task assigned to me by you. The uprising at Taxila has been subdued. There was lot more to be done there but why have I been called back so precipitously?" inquired Ashoka.

Maharaja, in a flattering tone, "I feel elated with your success at Taxila, my son!" King continued cautiously, ".....But there is a general feeling among the cadres that as per protocols I should have given my elder Prince the first chance to prove himself at Taxila. Therefore I have now decided to send Sushima to Taxila as Viceroy, to further continue the work from where you have left." Avoiding seeing Ashoka eye-to-eye, Maharaja further continued, "I have another very important task for you at Ujjain. The province of Malwa[16] is prosperous with growing agriculture and commerce, yet the revenue collection from there has been declining year after year. I want to understand the reason of this fall. I am sure that you, as Viceroy of Ujjain, will get into the bottom of things and fix this anomalous situation."

Ashoka could easily guess that these developments were the outcome of games played by the opposite camp. He, however, bowed his head in agreement to the King without any expression of discontent over Majesty's decision.

Jubilant elder Prince Sushima moved to the west as Viceroy of Taxila, and his bete-noir Prince Ashoka to Ujjain.

Time rolled. Though Ujjain was a priestly dominated place, yet Ashoka, with his canny intelligence and dexterous handling, made his way through. Being a tough taskmaster, he soon brought the administrative machinery in his grip, reigned the corrupt and plugged the leakages. The revenue collection improved considerably to the surprise of many but to the disappointment a few, especially the sacrificial Brahmins.

At Taxila, the priestly class got revived and stood up to rally behind their favourite Viceroy Prince Sushima. This was much to the dislike of Taxilans, who by nature were more egalitarian. The governance naturally suffered, for the fissures in the cadres. The situation, however, did not go out of control, for the presence of mighty Mauryan army at the command of the Viceroy.

At Pataliputra, Bindusara had been keeping poor health for quite some time. Despite being under the caring hands of *Rajvaidya*[26] and his queens, his condition worsened. Alarmed by the precarious situation, Radhagupta, the Prime Minister, summoned an emergency meeting of the council of ministers. In the assembly,

Radhagupta announced, 'Maharaja's condition is very serious. While we pray for his early recovery and long life, we need to be prepared for any eventuality. Maharaja has not declared the name of his Crown Prince for the smooth succession. In this scenario we must call Prince Ashoka from Ujjain who is better experienced in governance and recommend to Maharaja to declare him the Crown Prince.'

While a majority of ministers supported Radhagupta's proposal Khallataka, the second minister stood up in rage and said vociferously, "No Sir! I disagree with your proposal. As per the dictum of *Arthashastra*[5] the eldest prince must be made the Crown Prince. Therefore, Prince Sushima who is second to none must be declared the Crown Prince." There were voices in Khallataka's support also.

Radhagupta interrupted, "Honorable Ministers! Prince Sushima is yet to go a long way. He, in my opinion, has not sufficiently matured to lead this vast land of *Aryavarta*. He exhibits juvenile traits. Once in a council meeting, to draw my attention, he hit on my head mockingly. This was an unbecoming behaviour on part of a prince towards the Prime Minister of the state."

Amidst the loud commotion, Khallataka walked out of the meeting with his supporters. Brahmin court was equally agitated and messengers were rushed by Khallataka to recall Sushima from Taxila. Meanwhile Vitashoka[41], the womb brother of Ashoka, hurried personally to Ujjain with his loyal soldiers to bring Ashoka to Pataliputra. Ashoka was regularly keeping himself updated about Pataliputra through his spy net, and was ready with his five hundred strong band of soldiers. As Vitashoka broke the latest news to Ashoka, the first rays of sun next morning fell on Ashoka's horses racing on the dusty road to Pataliputra. The distance of about one hundred *yojana*[13] between Ujjain and Pataliputra was covered by him swiftly in fifteen days.

Ashoka, Vitashoka and Radhagupta entered the King's Chamber. Bindusara lay in bed in a critical state, flanked by *Rajvaidya* on his bedside. His eyes were half-open. Seeing Ashoka, Bindusara went pale. Radhagupta softly uttered, "Maharaja! Prince Ashoka is here, you may pronounce him as the Crown Prince."

Bindusara tried to raise his head and as he could barely manage to mumble, "The Crown Prince…" his head dropped and eyes rolled back. The sentence remained incomplete. He was no more, and he left with an open fate for Patliputra.

Canny Radhagupta immediately called for an emergency meeting of council of ministers and made the announcement, "I inform the council with profound grief the passing away of our beloved Maharaja." After a brief silence he continued, "Before Maharaja departed for heavenly abode he declared that Ashoka be made the Crown Prince."

Sushima, on his way from Taxila, was still far away from the Capital Pataliputra. Amidst the voices of dissent, Ashoka occupied the throne with the support of his cohorts and ample blessings of his mother Queen Subhadrangi. Going strictly by the book, Ashoka had superseded his elder half-brother Sushima.

The road to the future for him, however was not smooth. His journey for the next four years was blood soaked. All his half-brothers opposed him, for his individualistic style of functioning and his fiery impulsive nature. He knew that keeping them alive would be a threat to him. Ashoka with his full command over army and the treasury became strong enough to slay all of them one by one Devaka, Ruchika, Tritsus…including the eldest and the heir Sushima only sparing his real brother Vitashoka. Sushima's pregnant wife fled to Nepal saving her life and giving birth to Sushima's son Nigrodha there who became a Buddhist monk at a very young age.

Ashoka, after fortifying his throne from all sides, formally coronated himself assuming the title *Priyadarshi*[22]. He became 'Maharaja Priyadarshi Ashoka'.

Priyadarshi Ashoka continued his journey as Maharaja of the vast land of *Aryavarta*. Borders of his empire were fairly secured except the one with Kalinga, the region to the south of Pataliputra. Kalinga was bound by the two mighty rivers Mahanadi and Godavari to its north and south, and on its eastern boundary was the Sea of Kalinga. Kalinga with Toshali as its capital was an independent, strong and prosperous region. Even Ashoka's grandfather, and his father, could not conquer Kalinga. Pataliputra's successive attempts to subdue Toshali went in vain. Kalinga had a strong army and important ports secured by its powerful navy. Kalingans were the first to travel offshore to the southeast for trade. Kalinga was a strategic threat to the Mauryan Empire as it fell on the route from Pataliputra to the Indian Peninsula. Ashoka took this as a challenge and marched with his ominous army up to the bank of river Daya, a tributary of Mahanadi.

Ashoka sent his emissary to Maha Padmanabh, the King of Kalinga to agree to his terms. Kalingans who had never learnt to surrender, consecrated their weapons and moved their troops. The two armies faced each other at Dhauli, on the bank of river Daya. It was early morning on a windy day, when the fierce battle began. Loud battle cries, rumbling of drums, blowing of conches and sounds of trumpets broke the sky apart. Flashing swords pined for each other's blood. Kalingan army, though smaller in size, fought very bravely and took an initial edge. But soon the showering of deadly iron tipped arrows of the Maurayn infantry, helped by a favourable wind direction, reversed the battle scene. Their darting arrows hit the mahouts and cavalry riders of opponents. They were thrown off their elephants and horses. Without riders' control the animals moved wildly trampling their own soldiers. The dance of fury was in its full nakedness. By the end of the day, the battlefield was covered with heaps of mutilated strewn bodies of dead soldiers and animals. The water of river Daya, which was witness to gory battle, became red with the blood of humans and animals. Over a hundred thousand were dead, and nearly double the number lost their limbs and were taken prisoners.

Toshali fell under the loud wails of widows and cries of orphans. As the night fell, the howling of jackals and the hooting of hyenas feasting on the dead bodies at the battleground broke the eerie silence. The gloomy dawn next day saw flocks of vultures hovering over the sky and for many days that followed. The scene grew loathsome.

Ashoka, not normally given to emotions, was horrified and shaken witnessing the devastation and bedlam caused by the war. He could not sleep for many nights. He was so upset that he directed his troops to refrain from plundering and depredation of the hapless people of defeated Kalinga, which used to be a normal practice. When some of his commanders and ministers lauded him for his historic victory, he was not amused. This became a dramatic moment of his life. In search of peace of mind, he sought refuge in Lord Buddha. Ashoka drew closer to the community of Buddhist monks. He devoted his energy to the welfare of the people of his empire with no more sacrifices, no grand feasts and to use his army only for defense. He devoted himself to propagation of Buddhism, not only in *Aryavarta* but beyond, in foreign lands of Sri Lanka, Nepal, Thailand, China, Afghanistan, Syria, Egypt and Alexandria.

~

The Queens

Having a large number of queens in *antahpur*[3] was a privilege and status symbol of that era. Compared to his father who had sixteen queens, Ashoka had only five. Despite his enthusiasm for Buddhism, Ashoka did not forego the royal privilege of acquiring many wives during various stages of his life.

Devi was the first queen that Ashoka married when he was barely twenty years of age. When he was made the Viceroy of Ujjain on his journey to the west, Ashoka had a sojourn at Vidisha[37]. Vidisha gave a grand welcome to the Viceroy. Sukhvihar, the biggest of all the merchants undertook the major responsibility of extending hospitality to the Viceroy. The beautiful city was decorated like a bride, with strings of fresh flowers along the road and lovely *torans*[34] positioned at regular intervals. People along the road joyously welcomed, as Viceroy's party moved with Ashoka waving to them while sitting in the royal howdah of his elephant. Sukhvihar's young daughter, Devi led the group of maidens who received Ashoka at the splendid mansion where the Viceroy was hosted. Ashoka's eyes lay upon the fine, oval faced, tall, slim, youthful, radiant faced Devi, elegantly dressed for the occasion. While other girls were hesitant and shied away from the prince, Devi was confidently poised conducting the prince. That impressed Ashoka. There was a pleasing tête-à-tête between the two and it culminated into love at first meeting. Sukhvihar was pleased to discern the desire of the Viceroy. He happily gave his daughter in marriage to Prince Ashoka. Devi became Maha Devi and moved to Ujjain with Ashoka.

The merchant and agriculturist class in the Malwa region advocated that sound agriculture and trade are the backbone of prosperity of any state. They believed that the sacrificial Brahmanical order was a huge impediment to it. As a consequence, majority of them took shelter under Lord Buddha who preached nonviolence as way of life. Devi being the daughter of a merchant naturally became an ardent follower of Buddhist order. Prince Ashoka and Devi, though shared a close loving bond, Devi could not convince Ashoka to join the order. She had to wait until the Kalinga war when Ashoka had a change of heart.

Ashoka had two children from Devi, a son Mahendra and a daughter Sanghmitra. When Ashoka went back to Pataliputra she did not follow him despite many persuasions and remained at Vidisha. For her, Ujjain and Vidisha were places of peace away from strife of Pataliputra. She nurtured her children at Vidisha as apostles of Buddhism. Ashoka later sent both as his ambassadors with a delegation to Ceylon for propagation of Buddhism along with a sapling of the Bodhi tree[7]. The sapling planted by them in Ceylone soon took its roots and grew as a clone to the original Bodhi. The siblings also succeeded in rooting and spreading Buddhism in that country. Devi, remaining in Vidisha, became instrumental in constructing great Buddhist *Viharas*[38] at Vidisha and Sanchi[27].

Devi's refusal to move to Pataliputra entailed Ashoka to marry someone who was befitting his stature and become *Agramahisi*[1], the chief queen of the emperor. Ashoka, after his coronation, had a formal marriage with **Asandhimitra**, the princess of a small principality of Assandh, four *yojans* southwest of the city of Karnal, the historical city founded by Karna[12] in the Mahabharata. Asandhimitra was fine looking, mature, calm and composed in her conduct. Ashoka was deeply touched by her pure beauty and earnestness. She lived with Ashoka in the imperial palace and gained the status of *Agramahisi*, the first lady of the empire. Asandhi was a faithful companion and a trusted adviser of the king. She stood by him throughout her life, in every trial and tribulation of governance. The Emperor banked on her for sound advice for all critical issues before taking any action. When the Emperor decided to attack Kalinga, his *Agramahisi* differed as she did not like the idea. Ashoka later realized his mistake of not going with Asandhi's advice and deeply regretted it. Asandhi did not bear any children but took motherly care of Ashoka's other children.

Asandhimitra adorned Ashoka with her company for thirty long years. She, in her later years, was keeping poor health and was attended to by a charming, young and skilful caretaker **Tishyarakshita**. He helped her make way to Ashoka's *antahpur* by becoming his queen just before Asandhi's death.

Ashoka's Queen **Karuvaki**, a fisherman's daughter, came from Kalinga. When Kalinga was not a part of Magadhan Empire, Ashoka crossed the border of Kalinga and stayed there incognito. He was curious to have firsthand information of this land and its people, which Chandragupta and Bindusara, with all their might, could not conquer. Ashoka, in his adventurous spirit, moved deeper into the country and reached the turbulent Bay of Kalinga. While staying there in a camouflaged camp he met this beautiful girl of the fisherman. Her cheerful and carefree demeanour attracted Ashoka. Karuvaki's inexhaustible energy and feisty temperament appeared to be springing from the sea she lived by. Their casual meetings by the seaside turned into close acquaintance. Ashoka gradually drowned into her deep laughing eyes. They were married, and Karuvaki came to Pataliputra with him.

The still air and restrained ambience of *antahpur* were not to the liking of young Karuvaki. Her original spontaneity and witty manners were subdued in the regal environment. Once, when Ashoka inquired why she didn't appear to be at her best of spirits, she replied, "I ruled the sea with my laughter, which has faded away in these somber surroundings. It appears that I am constantly under watchful eyes. This is suffocating at times."

Ashoka, knowing her nature, later got a magnificent palace constructed for her at Kausambi, five *yojans* from the city of Prayagraj. She was happy to gain her exclusive space away from imperial Pataliputra. Having ample time at her disposal, generous Rani Karuvaki devoted herself to the activities for the welfare of the people. Ashoka undertook a series of benevolent measures on the advice of Karuvaki. She was the mother of a very promising son, Prince Tivala, who unfortunately died in his youth and could not outlive Ashoka.

Ashoka's Queen **Padmavati** died very early, within a short period of having her son Kunala. Kunala was raised by the childless *Agramahisi*, Asandhimitra. He had strikingly beautiful eyes. Kunala, thus was given the name, which in Sanskrit, stands for eagle 'the bird with beautiful eyes'. He was the much loved son of Ashoka. The emperor declared him as the Crown Prince of the Empire.

~

The Youngest Rani

(Tishyarakshita standing in front of the mirror in dressing room of Queen Asandhimitra.)

Tishyarakshita lost in admiring her inimitable beauty in the cheval mirror placed in Queen Asandhimitra's quarters. Tishyarakshita was the leader of the group of attendants in service of the queen. Being the queen's chosen one, she was permitted to dress herself with cosmetics and ornaments. Adorned with the necklace and earrings gifted by the queen and even with minimum makeup, she looked strikingly sensuous. She smiled to herself. There was a hint of vanity in her aslant smile. The woman in the mirror whispered, "In what manner do I appear less than the regality?"

Her thoughts slipped back to the hamlet in Ujjain where she lived with her father before coming to Pataliputra. Her father was a smalltime surgeon and she assisted him in his daily procedures. Soon, she mastered the skills with nursing. As her grasp was impressive, her father encouraged his beautiful daughter to join a local dancing *gurukul*[11]. She quickly learned her dance steps and became an accomplished *kathak* dancer. Suddenly Tishyarakshita's chain of thought was broken by the call, "Tishya…." Asandhimitra called her from adjoining chamber.

She rushed to the queen's chamber and bowed before the chief queen who was in her bed. "How are you feeling now *Agramahisi*?" she inquired.

"Better! Come, help me sit."

Tishyarakshita placed a long round pillow behind the *maharani*[15] for support. She picked up potion prepared by *Rajvaidya* and stood by the side of the queen. She knew that the queen disliked its taste. Tishyarakshita held the cup close to queen's lips who gulped it in one go. Despite the bitter taste that the potion had left in her mouth, she said with a smile, "You are always a great help, Tishya!"

Tishyarakshita beamed with a broad smile.

"Tishya, you look charming as always," observing her raptly Asandhi continued, "I am going to tell the Maharaja that you are not only a skillful nurse but also a graceful dancer." The Queen closed her eyes.

In the evening at sunset, the emperor made his entry into the queen's chamber. This had become almost his daily routine since Asandhimitra became bed-ridden with illness. *Agramahisi* welcomed the King with a broad smile. Tishyarakshita bowed to him. Ashoka was pleased to see Asandhimitra's smile as he sat on her bedside.

"You look lively today, my Asandhi. There appears to be improvement in your health," said Ashoka fondly holding the queen's hand.

Asandhimitra's smile broadened, "Yes my Lord! This is largely the effect of good care by Tisharakshita." Maharaja threw a glance towards Tishyarakshita, who was poised in the King's presence. Asandhimita continued, "And you know your Majesty, Tishya, apart from being an expert nurse, is an accomplished dancer."

"That is nice!" remarked Ashoka giving the young maiden a closer look.

"Maharaja, if you agree, we may have a dance session in the palace courtyard. We may invite a few selected choreographers along with our Tishya to give the performance," proposed Asandhimitra.

Ashoka nodded with a smile, "If that makes my Asandhi happy, I am all for it. Choose the date and convey it to the Minister of Culture for making arrangements." Ashoka got up saying, "Do take good care of yourself."

Tishyarakshita was thrilled, yet kept her exuberance from surfacing to her face. As the King left, Asandhimitra said, "Rehearse your dance steps Tishya, you are going to share the stage with best of the dancers of Pataliputra."

Tishya nodded with a sheepish smile.

~

Vasanta[36] Poornima evening was fixed up for the cultural event. A huge stage was set in the large palace courtyard. Arrangements of proper lighting and seating for the aristocracy were made with utmost care. List of attendees was limited, with senior Ministers accompanied by their wives, Prince Kunala and his wife Kanchanmala. Maharaja persuaded the Maharani to join the festivities, who was not in the best of her health. The program was deliberately kept short and crisp, with a handful of performers keeping *Agramahisi's* health condition in view.

On the Eastern horizon a full moon appeared, bigger than usual in the company of twinkling stars. Gentle breeze was loaded with the stimulating fragrance of *Vasanta* bloom. As the Maharaja entered in the courtyard and settled, performances began with a brief introduction by the narrator.

The entire session captivated the audience with the group and solo performances by elegant dancers accompanied by the *tabla*[30], *pakhavaj*[24], *manjira*[17] and flute. Tishyarakshita's performance was the last one. She had practiced hard for the day, stealing time from her sleeping hours. The result of her hard work and talent was alive on the stage. With the beats of the *tabla* and melody of the *sarangi*[28] she took the stage by a storm. Her footwork and moves were simply enrapturing. The graceful swirls of her lithe tall figure, with tantalizing facial expressions in rhythm of the *taal*[29] were mesmerizing. It was astounding for everyone including the emperor, who did not expect it to be so out of the world. As she ended, there was absolute silence for few moments before everyone came out of the trance. There was spontaneous applause with continuous clapping. Ashoka stood up and profusely praised the artists with a special mention of Tishyarakshita. Gifts were showered upon the performers.

The event was over but the emotion it left lingered in the minds of spectators. Tishyarakshita, naturally, was on cloud nine. She could see that her dance steps have left an imprint on Ashoka's heart. She became mildly informal in her conversations with the queen, and at times even with the King. Coming to know that Tishyarakshita loved outdoors, Asandhimitra allowed her to receive training in horse riding and archery. Asandhimitra arranged good trainers of the Magadhan army for her, of course with the nod by the emperor. Soon she found a place among the good archers of Pataliputra.

Kings have a general propensity to be lured towards the fairer sex, no matter how old they get. This could be for their position, power and access to plenty. Ashoka was no exception to this. Asandhimitra's health issues required Ashoka to frequent her quarters. Tishyarakshita was now an added reason to it. While sitting in the queen's chamber, his eyes roved behind Tishyarakshita. Tishya gauged it, and even Asandhimitra's female instincts read it. Ashoka, however maintained the dignity of a king and his Buddhist restraint. With drooping health, *Agramahisi* became increasingly confined to her chamber.

Crown prince Kunala's deep concern made him visit *Agramahisi* more often. She was more than a mother to him as Asandhimitra never let him feel the absence of his own mother Padmavati. Tishyarakshita was nursing the mother queen during one of his calls on her. Asandhi warmly told Kunala, "She is Tishya from Ujjain. I owe a lot to her for taking good care of me."

"Yes I know. She gave a magical dance performance the previous day," replied Kunala.

Tishya bowed to *yuvaraj*[44] throwing *a* bewitching smile.

Asandhi and Ashoka were soul mates in the true sense. Ashoka's wellbeing was always foremost on her mind and for Ashoka she was the most valuable company. On the folowing day, when the king was sitting with queen, she expressed, "Majesty! I have lived my life to the fullest. It appears that the time to drop the curtain is drawing close," she continued with a pause, "I take liberty to propose you to marry Tishya before my eyes are closed."

For Ashoka this was an unexpected suggestion from *Agramahisi*. He gave a bewildered look. Asandhi continued, "Devi remains at Vidisha[37], and Karuvaki is happy at Kausambi. I suggest you make Tishyarakshita your *Agramahisi* after me. She has all the qualities to be your Maharani, and your companion."

Ashoka kept mum for a while. He always valued Asandhimitra's assessments but this was an awkward moment for him. Tishya had sufficiently cast her spell on the Maharaja by now. He barely managed to say before leaving, "You are going to live long my Asandhi."

Tishyarakshita was listening the conversation from the neighbouring chamber. A mysterious smile appeared across her face. Young Tishya had no affinity with the old, rough skinned

King. She was elated with the thought of being the Maharani of *Arayavarta*.

Within a couple of days, Tishyarakshita became Ashoka's youngest queen. She continued to serve Asandhimitra in her deteriorating condition until one morning when she did not wake up from her sleep. Ashoka remained very sad for many days that followed. He slowly came to terms with the loss abiding by the saying of Tathagata[31], 'Decay is inherent in all compound things.'

The beaming new *Agramahisi* could often be seen now by the side of the emperor, on special occasions in the court or sitting on the royal elephant while he travelled in the countryside.

~

The Crown Prince

The Crown Prince was deeply engrossed in his flute. He was sitting under the canopy at the eastern end of the large courtyard. The royal courtyard was enclosed at human height, by elegantly carved stone-walls. Trees were pruned carefully to restrict their wild growth. Shrubs over the lush green well-mowed grass were manicured with fine filigree of flowers. The creepers climbed the highly ornamented slender columns warily erected for their support. The rays of the setting sun falling over vegetation and structures looked as if they were painted in crimson. Chirping of birds created pure harmony with the sweet melody of Kunala's flute. His eyes were close, lips on embouchure and fingers deftly dancing on the flute.

The euphony in the air touched Maharaja Ashoka's ears, who was taking an evening stroll in the corridors around the courtyard. Maharaja walked towards *yuvaraj* and quietly stood by his side. He did not want an interruption. Kunala was absorbed playing the evening raga *Marwa*[18] unmindful of the king standing by his side. Suddenly the prince opened his eyes and saw the Maharaja. He instantly stood up and bowed to the king. There was someone else also in the royal courtyard who was intently watching the father and son from behind the veil of creepers.

Ashoka smiled and placed his hand on *yuvaraj's* shoulder, "You have mastered your notes Kunala." Kunala smiled with a twinkle in his beautiful eyes.

Ashoka continued, "I am happy that you are becoming independent in taking your decisions. Kanchanmala is a nice girl, you have chosen."

"I am satisfied that you have liked my choice dear father," said Kunala.

Ashoka sauntered with his son towards the corridors covered on both sides with a thick curtain of hanging creepers. He said, "Kanchanmala has to be groomed in the matters of governance. One day she has to pick up the mantle of *Agramahisi*."

Kunala looked at his father with inquisitive eyes. Ashoka elucidated, "Yes my dear son, I am now into my twilights. You are the future protagonist for wellbeing of *Aryavarta* and its people. You have to lead them further on the path of Buddha."

"This great land of *Aryavarta* will continue to flourish in your hands Maharaja. I am happy to move on Buddha's path under your able guidance."

"My dear Kunala, the wheel of time continues to rotate. The old has to leave, to give space to the new. Look, Asandhi has gone and one day I too shall pass. You have to move out of your comfort zone, to be in the midst of governance, of course without drifting from Buddha's path," asserted Ashoka.

Tishyarakshita had been following Kunala for some time. His enchanting persona, youthful elegance, and above all, his captivating eyes allured her. There was a significant age gap of over four decades between old Maharaja and his young *Agramahisi*. She had no attraction for the king except that he was a King. Her status was braided with the King. Her heart, however, continuously yearned for a glimpse of Prince Kunala. At times, she surreptitiously followed him to the courtyard. That day, she was watching Kunala from behind the clump of creepers. She was stunned for a moment by the sudden entry of the King. But she was hardy. Maintaining her composure, she slithered closely behind the father and son hiding behind the natural curtain of the vegetation, and could eavesdrop.

Tishyarakshita brought up in Ujjain in a Brahmanic environment, as such had an intrinsic anti Buddhist streak in her. She detested that every facet of life here was replete with Buddha. For her this was a way towards inaction, not suited for the royalty. The King and the Crown Prince parroting Buddha too often appeared to her a waste of precious moments of one's life. She, however did not allow her predisposition surface.

Back in the queen's chamber, Kunala's thoughts did not leave Tishyarakshita. It had almost become an obsession for her. The very next day she found Kunala playing another raga sitting in the same corner of the royal courtyard. The royal courtyard was an exclusive place for royals. No one other than the king, queens and princes were allowed entry except on certain special occasions. Tishyarakshita was overjoyed to see him. The pure notes emanating from the flute of *yuvaraj* mixed with their sweet echo were mesmerising. This time shedding her hesitation she walked up to *yuvaraj* with hastened steps. As the queen came closer, Kunala opened his eyes and stopped playing. He got up and bowed to *Agramahisi*.

"Why did you stop Kunala! Your flute was suffusing nectar in the air," sonorously said Tishyarakshita.

"It is all by the grace of Tathagata and blessings of elders, dear Mother."

Tishyarakshita got ticked-off by *yuvaraj* addressing her as mother. She held his arm and gently made him sit by her side.

"Your play of flute is enticing Kunala, as if Krishna himself is playing through you," said Tishya chirpily throwing a beguiling glance.

Kunala folded his hands beholding the sky said, "I am honoured, mother Tishya."

"Why do you address me mother? Am I that old to be called mother?"

"You are the *Agramahisi* of Maharaja and the mother queen of entire *Aryavarta*," Kunala averred.

"Oh! That is for the protocol, symbolic and ceremonial. I am too young to be your mother," Tishyarakshita got closer to Kunala.

Kunala was puzzled. He stood up and bowed with folded hands, "I have some engagements in the palace. May I leave Maharani?"

Yuvaraj left leaving Tishayarakshita somewhat fazed. She was self-assured of her enticing beauty and was sure of captivating anyone with her charm. But, the bait appeared to be ineffective on the prey. She kept musing, 'Maybe he was feeling shy. Kanchanmala is comely but not as matchless. She is young, so am I,' Tishyarakshita kept pondering over the ways to entrap Kunala's heart.

Physical attraction apart, there was also a political reason behind her overtures. Tishyarakshita had a lurking fear that once the old King would be gone her fate would be unknown. She will not remain *Agramahisi* anymore. With Kunala in her fold she could continue to occupy the central space. Being the all-powerful young and crafty first lady of the limitless empire she had plenty of wherewithal and time on her side. Her head and heart acted simultaneously. She began to nurture her rapport with the disgruntled ministers, unhappy officials and resentful Brahmins. Minister Khallataka was the foremost among them. He was the man who had supported Sushima against Ashoka to be the Crown Prince. With his masterly tact, he could still save his post of the

Senior Minister, only after Prime Minister Radhagupta after Ashoka became the King. He was never happy in his heart for too much Buddhism influencing the state. He was for the army to be as aggressive as it was during the days of Kalinga war. The Mauryan army had not fought any major war after Kalinga. The cutting edge of the army had reduced, soldiers were more relaxed and weapons were getting rusted without vigorous exercises. This dormancy was due to Buddhism becoming the state religion for many years, where the army was diluted to merely defend the boundaries and not for invasion. The governing philosophy of Ashoka had been that while fear of a mighty national army would deter the aliens, the true compassion in intensions would bring about a change of heart of the adversary. To Tishyarakshita, this kind of philosophy appeared a utopia, far away from reality …. And she was too realist.

Tishyarakshita was on a hunt for an opportunity to be in the exclusive company of Prince Kunala. She received information that Kanchanmal was not too well, for the change in the weather. The King was also out on his tour to Sarnath for a few days. She sent across communication to Kunala, through her confidant attendant Sakula, to join her for an evening feast in her quarters. On the day of the feast Kanchanmala being unwell could not join the repast. *Yuvaraj* was reluctant to go alone, but then *Agramahisi's* invitation was a command that he could not circumvent.

Yuvaraj was escorted to the guests' chamber. As *Agramahisi* entered, he came forward and bowed to greet her in respect, "My apologies Maharani, Kanchanmala could not come, due to her ill health."

Tishyaraksha was glad to find that things were moving as per her wish. Feigning disappointment, Tishyarakshita said, "Oh! It is my hard luck, but never mind. Let the *yuvarani* nurse herself to health."

The prince, attired in off-white silken robes with his buoyant youthful frame, well-chiseled face and captivating eyes brought a gentle whiff of blooming jasmines with him. There was compelling attractiveness in his sight and the way he carried himself. For Tishyarakshita this was the most intoxicating moment.

The magnificent guest chamber was carefully embellished for welcoming the special visitor. The sweet aroma of burning *loban*[14] was floating in the air. Tishyarakshita, in a vibrant blue attire looked like a sensuous celestial *apsara*[4] to the likes of Urvashi or Rambha. Her perfect dancing profusely reflected in her sinuous gait, harmonious with the tinkling of her anklets. The Queen was all set to ignite the passion in the prince, like the nymph Menaka[40] inflamed in Sage Vishwamitra[39] with her charm.

An entourage of attendants entered and laid the bonanza of dishes for feasting. The titillating aroma of spices and herbs suppressed the sweet fragrance of the smouldering *loban*. The attendants moved out of the chamber as instructed by the Rani that she would herself be serving the guest. *Yuvaraj*, though born and brought up in regal affluence, was not used to such rollick opulence.

Tishyarakshita's visage and postures were making him uncomfortable, yet he kept the courteous smile on his face intact. To engage the Rani he looked at the great spread in front of him and remarked, "You took too much pain for such an elaborate banquet, revered Maharani."

"Which one would you prefer to start with, my dear Kunala?" asked Tishyarakshita pouring extra sweetness in her voice.

"Everything looks so divine, we may start with any item, Maharani," replied Kunala.

Tishyarakshita started serving the items one after the other until Kunala was more than full. But Tishyarakshita had kept the *payasam*[21] for the finale. She was astute enough to know that Kunala will not refuse the *payasam*, the dish served to Gautama by Sujata after which he attained enlightenment.

"Oh! The *payasam*!" exclaimed Kunala and took it with full reverence.

Tishyaraksha was amorously gaping at Kunala while he was eating. The company of a young prince was elevating her spirit that had jaded living with the old and withered King. Her part of the feast was yet to begin.

She suddenly asked Kunala, "What does the prince feel looking at me?"

"You are beautiful," said Kunala with a frown.

"Beautiful?" laughingly she said, "Just beautiful?"

"What more can I say?"

"You can say. Is the beauty of Kanchanmala more than mine?" asked Tishyarakshita desperately moving closer to the prince.

An uncomfortable Kunala said, "This kind of comparison is sinful, Maharani!"

"Sin? Why is it a sin?"

"Because you are my mother."

"Mother? In what manner am I your mother? Never!" hissed Tishyarakshita.

Kunala was stunned, "What are you saying, Maharani? You are the *Agramahisi* of the Maharaja, my father. Therefore you are my revered mother."

"Don't call me mother. In what way am I lesser than Kanchanmala?" shrieked Tishyarakshita.

Getting up from the couch Kunala said, "Maharani, the truth is that you are my mother. Tathagata will certainly dawn clarity to your mind."

Tishya retorted, "Was Tathagata himself clear in his mind? To him, women stood second to men. He did not have any belief in us. He explicitly said that without the women, Sangha would survive thousand years. Admitting women to it shall reduce its life to five hundred years. Isn't it a shear insult to women? When Tathagata himself was discriminatory, in what stance can one compare the commoners?"

"Honorable Maharani, you appear to be disturbed for some reason. You need some rest. Please allow me to leave," *Yuvaraj* bowed to the Queen and walked out of the chamber.

The prey had slipped away from the predator. Tishyaraksha stood up with a racing heartbeat, blood gushing into her head. Tishyarakshita thought, 'Is Kunala greater than Rishi Vishwamitra or am I less a nymph than Menaka?' She had seen men dancing to her tunes. She had never experienced such downright rejection. She was deeply humiliated. Completely exhausted she managed to walk up to her bed and collapsed without changing her attire.

The Rani remained in her bed until the sun moved up in the sky next day. Sakula smelt that something had gone awfully wrong between the Rani and *yuvaraj* in the previous night.

Sakula came by the Rani's bedside and said, "Noble Maharani, it is late in the day now. You appear to be unwell."

The queen tried to regain her poise and got out of bed with a little effort. She remained morose the entire day. She continued to remain cheerless and confined to her chamber for the next few days. Her hurt grew deeper with every passing day. She was like a wounded tigress hunting for revenge.

~

Crown Prince Moves To Taxila

Taxila[32]the capital of the far western province of the empire always remained at a distance from Pataliputra. Its proximity with Iran and Bactria often instigated a rebellious mindset in the state. This was subdued with the might of the Magadhan army. Ashoka had tactfully handled the Taxila revolt during his younger days. This time the North West was raising its voice once again. Though the immediate threat had not surfaced, yet the situation needed to be contained before it brewed into a revolt.

The King, after prolonged deliberations with his council of Ministers, decided to depute *yuvaraj* as the Viceroy of Taxila. This, to his mind, was a necessary stepping-stone to the throne of Pataliputra. There was, however a lurking fear in Ashoka's heart about the safety of Kunala as the campaign was likely to take a couple of years. The Maharaja therefore deputed the best of his commanders, guards and attendants to accompany the Crown Prince. The Maharaja gave elaborate briefings to the *yuvaraj* about the society and geopolitical vulnerabilities of the land. He relieved him with his final words, "Exercise your wisdom. Take good care of you and *yuvarani*. May Tathagata lead your way."

It was early in the morning when the large contingent set out on a long, arduous journey. The convoy was led by armed war elephants with heavily armed warriors, followed by swift horsemen holding spears in their fists and shields hanging on their sides. The procession ended with decorated war chariots and finally an unending row of foot soldiers in their glittering uniforms.

The send-off was ceremonial. *Yuvaraj* and *yauvarani* were mounted over the royal elephant. A huge mass of people congregated along both sides of the road. Among the crowd were young lads, lively girls, street urchins and grown-ups, all attired in the best of their colourful dresses. They were waving, shouting and pushing each other to get a good glimpse of their young *yuvaraj* and *yuvarani*. Amidst the loud play of drums, trumpets and the holy conches, the contingent slowly marched out of the city's premises.

The caravan traversed parallel to the river Ganga during the initial part of its journey, crossing the river close to Kashi[13]. It travelled across the river Saryu and then Gomti while passing through Ayodhya, Mathura and Indraprastha. Moving by the side of thick forests, villages, agricultural lands, camping during the nights close to rivers or water bodies for the troops to relax and rejuvinate.

The journey was a novel experience for the royal couple. It was an opportunity to understand the diverse land and interact with its populace of the kingdom. The caravan reached Punjab after travelling for close to two months. The lush green agricultural fields welcomed them. People of Punjab were friendly, frank and appeared less ritualistic.

On reaching Taxila the royal assembly was received by the council of ministers, local commanders, priests and high officials led by Dipavasana, the Chief Minister of the province. After the customary welcome ceremony, Dipavasana explained to the *yuvaraj* the causes behind the recent unrest. He told that they have arrested three *Yavanas*[42] who were plotting against the native culture and governance. *Yuvaraj* intently listened to the prolonged briefings.

Viceroy asked the Chief Minister to declare a date for the trial of these *Yavanas*. On the day of trial, the *Yavanas* were summoned in the shackles to the heavily guarded Viceroy's Court. All of them were good-looking, well-built young men in their early thirties. They were well educated in the fields of art, architecture and political science. Proceedings began with reading of the charges against the accused.

The Viceroy asked the one who was senior most in age, "What made you to undertake a campaign against the empire? Are you unaware that such an act attracts capital punishment according to our laws?"

Yavana replied without getting perturbed, "Your Majesty, the reason lies in the cultural roots of this land that are very different from far off Magadha. People's hearts here are closer to Bactria. Keeping it under Pataliputra is not justified."

The Viceroy was somewhat surprised to observe the conviction of a man that he wasn't afraid of the looming death sentence upon him. Viceroy repeated, "You may be awarded the death penalty for instigating citizens against the state."

The *Yavana* remained unperturbed and said, "Sir, this is at the discretion of the court, we have to accept. But whatever we feel, we have submitted."

In normal course, the court would have passed the verdict against them immediately. But *yuvaraj's* curiosity was raised by the honesty of their cause. He raised a query, "What is so great about your culture which you find lacking in the native thought?"

The man replied, "Honorable sir, the state spends its considerable time, precious resources and energy on religion, which could otherwise be rightfully employed to the welfare of the people. Coming to our architecture, how grand is it compared to the local architecture which is simple, modest and lacks grandeur?"

Yuvaraj smiled and said, "No doubt, your focus on outward grandeur is visible in your work. You very well see the physical form but you miss the subtlety behind it; you miss the essential spirit in its backdrop. You must have observed the images of Buddha carved by the local artisans."

"Yes sir ample. We see the quintessential smiling Buddha everywhere."

"Do you think that these are just the smiling faces of Buddha. I may clarify to you that these are not merely physical images. These are the images of someone who is deep in meditation. These are the statues of *dhyana*[10]. They reflect the inner beauty and the non-violent spirit of a human being. These may not resemble the true face of Buddha, but the face of someone who has deep compassion in heart for all beings. If you look at it more reflectively you may sense its infiniteness."

The *Yavana* remained silent.

As the *yuvaraj* continued with his conversation, the *Yavana* appeared to be losing his ground.

Yuvaraj persisted, "The Maharaja has chosen the path shown by Buddha. Violence and the use of force is his last resort. You have talked about us wasting precious resources on religion. Do you not waste your energy and wealth on wars, bloodshed and intrigues? Does that help the common man in any manner? The Maharaja could have extended his empire beyond Hindukush with the might of his army but he chose the path of friendship and peaceful coexistence. He conquers with heart."

Yavanas were stunned by the innate beauty of *yuvaraj's* words and his benign presence. They couldn't help but come to their knees out of veneration. *Yuvaraj* with angelic glitter in his eyes pronounced, "As the accused have realized the aberration in their thinking and appear to have a change of heart we may release them," he further inquired, "Do you desire to stay at Taxila or leave for your country?"

The trio said, "Your Majesty we would be grateful if we are permitted to continue our stay in Taxila. We intend to enrich our craft here with our renewed mindset. We resolve to remain loyal to the Maharaja and the state."

Yuvaraj was impressed by the bold straightforwardness of the *Yavanas*. However, a few members of the court were shocked at Viceroy's judgment as it was first of its kind where amnesty was granted to the aliens despite their secessionist overtures. The *yuvaraj* had the final word in the matter and they were released. Viceroy, however as an abundant caution, instructed his administration to keep them under their watch until their conduct is established beyond doubt.

Yuvaraj, though, was firm while he was in the court. Yet, later he became apprehensive that his father, the Maharaja, may not approve his judgment. He revered his father as his guru whose word was infallible to him. The King's agreement was the touchstone for him. He communicated his decision about *Yavanas* to the King, through messengers to Pataliputra.

~

The Queen's Vengeance

Tishyarakshita remained restless. Her sizzling love towards Kunala had been transformed into bitter hate. She continued to engineer her own lobby among ministers, Brahmins, bureaucracy and in army ranks not only at Pataliputra but also at far off Taxila. The King, who had mellowed with age, did not have a whiff of what was fomenting under his nose. Blinded by the beauty and charm of the pretentious young *Agramahisi*, the Maharaja could not gauge her evil motives.

Tishyarakshita detested everything that was Buddhist. She considered the sacred Bodhi Tree[7] at Uruvela[35], under which Buddha attained enlightenment, an ominous object. She attempted to destroy it through her tricks. The tree wilted for some time but was nursed back to health by the special care of the Maharaja's experts. The King, however, did not come to know the person behind the injury to the sacred tree.

Ashoka was also having frequent health issues. Some people related it with the wilting of the Bodhi Tree, others thought it was due to his beloved son Kunala being away from him. Despite the best care and treatment, his condition deteriorated. Gradually, his movements became restricted from his palace to the court, and then slowly confined to his palace and ultimately limited to his bed. His poor health was a cause of concern to everyone including the Maharani. Tishyarakshita's anxiety was mounted, as should anything happen to the Maharaja she would lose the position as *Agramahisi*, for which she was not immediately prepared. That would be a big loss to her status. The King's disease was mysterious in nature, the cause of which was not becoming clear to the medical experts engaged in his treatment.

With no solution in sight, the Maharani directed to find someone with similar symptoms in Magadh and adjoining areas. After a hectic quest, a roadside beggar was found having the same symptoms and was in a serious condition. He was brought to the palace. Tishyarakshita asked *Rajyavaidya*, "We will dissect this man to investigate the reason of his malady."

Rajyavaidya shivered with fear, "This man might die in the process, Noble Maharani. The Majesty will never agree taking an innocent's life to save his own."

The Maharani persisted, "The Maharaja's life is much more precious for the empire, than the life of this common man, who is soon going to die with this terminal disease. Who knows our surgery may save his life?"

The Maharani herself was trained in surgery under the apprenticeship of her father at Ujjain. She, with *Rajyavaidya* and his team, dissected the man. They saw that there were two large sized worms sitting at the urinary tract causing obstruction and severe infection. They removed the worms, but before they could complete the stitching, the man died. But, with the trial the team had gained enough confidence to undertake king's surgery.

The same procedure was carefully repeated with the Maharaja. Though the Maharaja was old but he was in a much better physical shape. The worms were removed from his abdomen and after cleaning, the surgical section was stitched back. The King remained unconscious for the next three days. These were worrisome moments. On the fourth day, the Maharaja opened his eyes. This was a heartening news for the people of Magadh. He, however, remained weak for about a fortnight, and slowly began gaining strength. The King profusely thanked everyone especially *Agramahisi* for assiduously working to save his life.

Even during those trying times of Maharaja's terminal illness did not erase Tishyarakshita's rancor against Kunala from her mind. Her unsettled revenge against Kunala kept biting her. Finally, an opportunity arrived. She intercepted the communication from Kunala to the Maharaja regarding his decision about the *Yavanas*. Ashoka was not in a condition to receive the message. *Agramahisi* knew that father would have appreciated his son's act as an act of wisdom. She thought of a highly sinister plan against *yuvaraj*. She summoned the senior minister Khallataka. The minister was discontented with the ways of governance and as such Maharani had developed good proximity with him

Khallataka bowed before the Maharani who was sitting alone in her chamber. She said, "*Amatya*, I have called you to discuss something vital. In many ways, yours and my thinking is similar. The state is wasting its precious revenue on raising *viharas, stupas*, religious tours and giving gifts to the monks. This money needs to be spent in better ways." Then she revealed the ominous plan she had woven in her mind to Khallataka.

Listening to her stratagem, even the man of toughness of Khallataka was shocked for a while and said, "Maharani, don't you think that we are running into a dangerous game?"

"*Amatya*, the Maharaja is seriously ill. He may or may not survive. After him, his son Kunala who is equally Buddhist will tow his father's line. That will not benefit the empire. Revenues will continue to diminish, the might of our army will further dwindle and our enemies will be raising their heads. We need to remove Kunala from the line of succession. We are trying to save the Maharaja's life, but then he will become too feeble after such illness to go against us even if he desires so. We must also explore a sound alternative before time slips out of our hands."

Khallataka, despite initial hesitation, agreed seeing the firmness on Rani's face. He drafted a letter on behalf of the Maharaja to the Chief Minister of Taxila, as conspired. He secretly arranged for the Maharaja's Royal Seal and authenticated the letter.

The Royal Order stated:

'The Maharaja expresses his severe displeasure against Prince Kunala over his act of granting amnesty to the Yavanas, the enemies of the state. This is construed an act of treason against the Empire. Therefore, the Maharaja orders that the Prince be stripped of the charge of the Viceroy of Taxila with immediate effect. Considering the gravity of his misconduct, the eyes of the Prince be torn off to set an example for others to refrain from such doings. Further action on the delinquent Yavanas be taken after a fresh trial by the court.'

The letter was sent to Taxila through the confidant messengers of Khallataka for delivery directly in the hands of the Chief Minister. In Mauryan administrative system, the Chief Minister of a province was given certain exclusive executive powers. The direct orders from the King to the Chief Minister without keeping the Viceroy in the loop were regular occurrence. So, receipt of direct order from the King did not surprise the Chief Minister. However, what surprised him was the content of the letter. Though he was supposed to act as directed, yet he went to the Viceroy and told him about the King's Order.

Kunala was not receiving any communication from the Maharaja for long. Sitting far away at Taxila, he was not aware of Ashoka's grave illness. Tishyarakshita had chocked the flow of information to Taxila. *Yuvaraj* had forebodings whether the King had approved his decisions or not. When he was told about the King's order, he remained quiet for a few moments and then said, "This being the King's order must be followed without delay, as per laid down rules and norms."

The Chief Minister insisted, "Your Excellency, though it is a Royal Order, yet I think we may seek clarification."

Kunala calmly replied, "It carries the Royal Seal, which no one except the Maharaja can use. He is wiser of us all. This I feel is the will of Tathagata and must be followed."

Kunala did not even make his Rani Kanchanmala aware of this order, for the fear that she would come in the way of execution of the order. Over two centuries ago, Prince Siddhartha had also not taken his Rani Yashodhara into confidence before leaving his palace in the night in the quest for nirvana.

The orders were executed next morning and the beautiful eyes of Prince Kunala were removed. It was extremely painful for the Prince, and also for the man who executed the orders and tore them off his body. When Kanchanmala came to know of it, she cried and collapsed in shock. With passage of time Kunala's wounds were somewhat healed and so was Kanchanmala's pain and agony.

Prince Kunala had now no purpose to stay in Taxila, and he decided to move back to Pataliputra. He, with his Rani, and a small group of companions quietly moved away from Taxila.

After the lengthy onerous journey, they reached the borders of Pataliputra. The beating of rain, heat and dust and the hardships of a prolonged journey had hardened their faces beyond recognition.

On their way, they came to know of the serious ailment of the Maharaja and his recovery. The news was a surprise to them.

Kunala and Kanchanmala left their companions outside the borders of the city before they entered the city. Both looked so ordinary that passers-by and pedestrians did not take notice of them. When they reached the palace, they requested for an audience with the Maharaja. The Maharaja, though weak after his recovery had begun attending the court. After a short wait, they were allowed to be in front of the Maharaja as common folks, a woman and her blind husband. As they kneeled, the King asked, "What brings you to me?"

Emotionally chocked Kunala could just manage to utter, "Maharaja…."

Ashoka recognized the voice of his beloved son with the only word he had uttered. But, for their ordinary look he said, "Your voice is like my Kunala!"

Prince gaining his composure replied, "Yes Holy Maharaja, I am your Kunala."

Utterly shocked Maharaja got up from his throne and walked up to the Prince. He touched Kunala's rugged face and the spot where there used to be two lovely eyes. He hugged him and cried bitterly, "Who did this to you?"

Kunala had calmed down by now, "It is a long tale Noble Maharaja!"

Ashoka suddenly realized that they were standing in the *darbar*[9] surrounded by his ministers. Royalty has never been expected to express their emotions like common folks in public domain. King restrained his emotional outburst. Kunala and Kanchanmal were brought to the royal quarters with full honours. Kunala narrated the long tragic saga to his father. He also, for the first time, recounted the events that followed his encounter with Maharani Tishyarakshita in the Royal Cortyard.

Inundated in the flood of his tears, the restless Maharaja wailed, "Why didn't you bring it to my notice right then? This was not fair on your part my Kunala. I wish I had known this. Tishyarakshita is going to face the consequences for her base conduct and the grievous injury she inflicted upon you and the irreversible damage caused to the Empire."

Kunala sensing his father's rage said, "Dear father, please do not grieve. What I underwent is the play of my own destiny. I feel it brought me closer to Tathagata. Please be soft on mother Tishyarakshita."

Ashoka said churlishly, "Leave it to me now!"

~

The Royal Verdict

Khallataka was present in the *darbar* when the Prince entered with his Rani. The minister was shaken upon knowing that the aggrieved couple standing in front of the King was Kunala and Kanchanmala. Khallataka realized that their game was over. Whatever happened in the court was immediately conveyed by him to the Maharani through Sakula. It was a shocking news for Tishyarkshita also and she fell silent.

Sakula, realizing the gravity of situation, suggested, "Maharani! It would be prudent for you, at this moment, to leave this place. You are in a delicate situation. It fills me with pain to tell you that the odds are much against you. There are many outside Magadh who support you, and would provide shelter to you. Keep away till the dust settles."

Tishyarakshita, gaining her composure, replied, "Sakula, I have not sinned and I am not scared. I am not one to run away, hiding in shame. I am prepared for any consequence."

Soon, the King's soldiers entered Maharani's quarters and arrested her. Khallataka, and others who joined their hands with them, were also detained. Tishyarakshita and Khallataka were brought to the King's court the next morning.

Without providing any background, the King said, "You are aware of the charges against you. You harbour polluted thoughts. You indulged in forgery, usurping the authority not vested in you and committed an extremely brutal act of violence against an innocent Prince. Do you plead guilty?"

Khallataka had become numb and was mute with the lurking fear of death on his face. Tishyarakshita, though not in the best of her looks, said fearlessly, "I do not plead guilty Maharaja. I have no polluted thoughts. My actions followed the urge natural to a young woman. I acted in accordance with what I felt was good for the state and its people. I have committed no wrong."

Amidst the surprised expression of courtiers, at the bold reply from Tishyarakshita, Ashoka pronounced the death sentence upon both his *Agramahisi* and *Amatya*. The Emperor avoided looking into the eyes of his Maharani after passing the verdict.

Before dawn, Tishyarakshita was brought to the gallows. The hangman had not used his gibbet for quite long, as nonviolence was the credo of governance of the state. It was his first time hanging such a young, beautiful, royal woman, who was the Maharani of the Empire. His hands shook with nervousness while tying the knot, and her noose remained lose. She squirmed much longer on the ligature before her soul departed her body. It was an agonizing death.

A pall of gloom had enveloped Ashoka, Kunala and Kanchanmala that night. Sleep was far away from their eyes. The King had many questions to himself. There was violence in his own abode that was seen as the sanctum of nonviolence. Then he sought solace in Tathagata's saying, "I have shown you the path. No one can cleanse the other. Purity and impurity are self-creation."

Epilogue-II

Tishyarakshita could not escape the felony on her part. Her life and her conduct raises many perplexing questions. Tishyarakshita was an ambitious woman from an ordinary lineage. Being ambitious attracts no delinquency.

There was big age gap between the old Raja and the young Rani. Though, the King had the other queens yet he took another, much younger than him. His Buddhist ideologies did not bar him from doing so. The Rani's attraction towards someone of her age is a natural instinct of a young woman. Her fault was that she fueled it with bold expression while many others would keep it to their hearts out of fear.

In the game of thrones it was common practice to kill or be killed. Tishyarakshita blinded innocent Kunala, and so did Ashoka by killing his ninety-nine brothers to capture Magadhan seat. Many of them would have been innocent. After the brutal killings and bloodshed of the Kalinga war, Ashoka took shelter in Buddha. The King adopted Buddhism as the State Religion. His favorite son Kunala happened to be more Buddhist than his father. Tishyarakshita daringly raised valid questions about spending the state's precious revenues over religious activities, a thought that was much ahead of its time. The most modern day secularist states have adopted the principle that the state shall not spend public funds on religious activities and on theological institutions.

Tishyarakshita stands out as a strong feminist. This is one of her behavioral traits that made her animus to Buddhism and Buddha who placed women second to men. She advocated against the passivity that the Buddhist way of life had seeped into Mauryan governance. Tishyarakshita's instinct, the Freudian Id, remained so predominant that no amount of Buddhist environment could transform her towards non-violence.

Kunala strangely allowing himself to be blinded so easily without conversing even with his queen does raise an eyebrow. Perhaps he was such a contented soul to be desirous of taking the mantle of emperor of the vast kingdom of *Aryavarta*. Nurturing a strong urge to be a full time ascetic, perhaps this came as an opportunity that became an escape route for him.

The events of the entire plot are over two millennia old. As such, there are varying versions where history and legend are interwoven. There is a 1941 Tamil film titled 'Ashok Kumar' in which Kunala is named Kunalam and Tishayrakshita as Thishayrakshai. The Tamil version was based on, a previously made 1925 silent Hindi film, 'Veer Kunala'.

The film Ashok Kumar is about Ashoka's son Kunalam, whom the Emperor's young wife lusts after. Shocked, he rejects her amorous advances, and like a proverbial woman scorned, she tells her husband that his son tried to seduce her. Enraged, the aging emperor orders his son to be blinded and banished. The condemned, but innocent, prince suffers and is reduced to beggary. Ultimately, the Buddha miraculously restores his sight and rights all wrongs except those committed by the young Rani. They lived happily thereafter.

Another version connects the blinding of Kunala with the conspiracy of Ashoka'a succession. Tishyarakshita had a son whom she desired to succeed the King, and orchestrated the game to remove Crown Prince Kunala from the way.

Lastly, Tishyarakshita's premonition that the Empire was getting weaker proved to be correct. The successors of Ashoka could not hold the throne to them for long. The Mauryans lost the mighty Empire within fifty years Emperor Ashoka's death.

End Notes-II

1. *Agramahisi*: The principal queen.

2. *Amitrochates*: Greek term in Sanskrit *amitraghata* meaning 'the slayer of foes'. Greek referred Bindusar as *Amitrochates*.

3. *Antahpur*: Women's quarters in the palace. Harem.

4. *Apsara*: Beautiful supernatural female beings in Indian mythology. Urvashi, Menaka, Rambha, Tilottama and Ghritachi are widely known *apsaras*.

5. *Arthashastra*: Ancient Indian Sanskrit treatise on state-craft, economic policy, military strategy and governance. Kautilya also known as Chanakya or Vishnugupta is credited as the author of the text.

6. *Aryavarta*: The abode of Aryans. The term for northern parts of the Indian subcontinent in ancient Hindu texts. The tract between Himalya and Vindhyan ranges and from the Eastern Sea (Bay of Bengal) to the Western Sea (Arabian Sea).

7. Bodhi Tree : Tree at Bodh Gaya under which Siddharth Gautama attained enlightenment, also called Bo Tree.

8. *Brahmin*: Member of highest *varna* (caste group) in Hindu society. Traditionally responsible for teaching and maintaining sacred knowledge.

9. *Darbar* : Royal court.

10. *Dhyana*: Seventh limb of Rishi Patanjali's eight fold path of yoga.

11. *Gurukul*: An education system prevalent in ancient India where pupils resided with their guru (teacher) till their education got completed.

12. Karna : The spiritual son of Sun god and princess Kunti in Hindu epic Mahabharata. An extraordinary warrior.

13. Kashi : Holy city, Varanasi in Indian state of Uttar Pradesh. City of Lord Shiva. Buddha gave his first sermon here after enlightenment.

14. *Loban*: Frankincense, aromatic resin obtained from the bark several species of trees, when burnt give pleasing aroma.

15. *Maharani*: The chief queen.

16. Malwa : The region of west-central India.

17. *Manjira*: Traditional percussion instrument in its simplest form, is a pair of small hand cymbals.

18. *Marwa raga*: Indian raga characterized as contemplative, representing gentle love. Overall mood of the raga is defined by the sunset.

19. Pataliputra : Situated on the right bank of Ganges at the confluence of rivers Ganga and Sone (Erannobos). Started with an Army camp established by Ajatshatru was built as a city by his son Udayin the ruler of Magadha. It remained as capital of Mauryans and several dynasties after them. Its modern name is Patna in the state of Bihar, India.

20. *Pandavas*: The five sons Pandu. The princes of the epic Mahabharata.

21. *Payasam*: A type of pudding from Indian subcontinent made by boiling milk, sugar and rice or vermicelli also known as *kheer*. Gautama Buddha after he became weak after

prolonged penance was offered *kheer* by milkmaid Sujata. After consuming it, he gained strength and that night he attained enlightenment to propagate the middle path.

22. *Priyadarshi*: The humane.

23. Punjab : The land of five rivers Jhelum, Chenab, Ravi, Sutlej and Vyas. Partitioned in year 1947 into Indian Punjab and Pakistan Punjab.

24. *Pakhavaj*: A barrel shaped, two headed drum, originated from Indian subcontinent.

25. Rajgriha : Ancient city surrounded by hills in the state of Bihar, India. It was the first capital of Kingdom of Mgadha, the state that eventually evolved into Mauryan Empire.

26. *Rajvaidya*: The royal physician.

27. Sanchi : Forty six kilometers northeast of Bhopal in state of Madhya Pradesh, India. Known for its Buddhist stupas.

28. *Sarangi*: Short necked string instrument, largely used in Punjabi and Rajasthani folk music. It most resembles the sound of human voice.

29. *Taal*: Literally means a clap or beat in rhythm.

30. *Tabala*: Pair of small hand drums fundamental to Hindustani music of India, Pakistan, Bangladesh and Nepal.

31. *Tathagata*: One of the honorific titles of a Buddha or a person who has attained perfection by following the path shown by Buddha.

32. Taxila : Known as *Takshashila,* the ancient capital of far west, Punjab. Thirty-two kilometer northwest of Islamabad, now

in Pakistan. The city said to have been founded by Bharata, younger brother of Rama of Ayodhya for his son Taksha.

33. The Great Indian Empire : The Indian land that was ruled by Mauryas that included modern day Pakistan and Bangladesh and parts of Nepal and Afghanistan but not extending to Kerala and Tamil Nadu.

34. *Toran*: Decorated gates.

35. Uruvela : Tiny village on the bank of Nairanjana River, now known as Bodh Gaya. Buddhist pilgrimage.

36. *Vasanta*: Also known as *Basant*, the spring season of Hindu calendar. The season occurs from mid March to mid May, *Chaitra* and *Vaishakh* months of Hindu calendar.

37. Vidisha : Sixty two kilometers northeast of Bhopal and eight hundred ninety kilometer from Patna. Administrative headquarter of Bhilsa during ancient period. Great Sanskrit poet Kalidasa's Meghdootam finds mention of the city.

38. *Vihara*: Buddhist monastery. Originally constructed to provide shelter to the monks during rainy season when it became difficult for them to lead the wanderer's life.

39. Vishwamitra : One of the most venerated rishis of Indian mythology. He was seduced by *apsara* Menaka.

40. Menaka, who succeeded in breaking Rishi Vishwamitra's penance.

41. Vitashoka : The womb younger brother of Ashoka from mother Subhaddrangi. Vitashoka means 'sorrow terminated' whereas Ashoka means 'without sorrow'.

42. *Yavana*: Term used for Greeks or other foreigners in early Indian literature.

43. *Yojana*: Measure of distance. One *yojana* is about twelve kilometers.

44. *Yuvaraj*: Crown Prince.

PHAEDRA

Characters-III

THESEUS : King of Athens

PHAEDRA : Theseus's wife, stepmother of Hippolytus

HIPPOLYTUS : Theseus's son by Hippolyta, the queen of Amazons

THE NURSE : Phaedra's favourite old nurse

ATTENDANTS : In service of Phaedra

COMPANIONS of Hippolytus

MESSENGER

IMAGES : Aphrodite and Artemis

Hippolytus-The Devotee of Artemis

At Troezen[15], in front of the house of Theseus, the King of Athens, stand statues of two Greek goddesses, one of Artemis[4] and another of Aphrodite[1]. Artemis is the goddess of animals, hunting and vegetation, of chastity, childbirth and preserver of the young. Aphrodite is associated with beauty, pleasure, passion and procreation, who could charm the gods and men alike.

Hippolytus, the son of Theseus is standing in front of the house with attendants.

Hippolytus to his companions, "Listen! Sing in the praise of the heavenly Artemis, the daughter of Zeus. We remain under her protective care."

Attendants sing in unison:

Hail! Hail! The girl divine!

Hail! Hail! The holy virgin!

Most beauteous, the daughter of Zeus[16] and Leto[9]!

Dwelling in the measureless sky,

In the golden mansion of father Zeus;

O the most beauteous of virgins living in Olympus[11]!

Hippolytus, holding a wreath in his hand in reverence to the statue of Artemis, said, "O my most beauteous virgin lady, I offer you this fresh wreath woven by me. Its flowers I plucked from the undefiled garden, where no shepherd dares to graze his flock, no gardener uses his iron tools to prune, watered only with waters from the river. Only those who have learnt the lesson of chastity from mother nature, and not from classrooms or from books, are allowed to gather flowers there. The impure are debarred," he continued, "O dear mistress, accept this coronal to swathe your golden tresses. I am buoyed to receive this rare privilege to exchange my words with you. However, I am unable to see your expressions."

The attendant said, "O King! I will not address you as 'Lord' as it is reserved for the gods alone. Would you care to take an advice?"

"Yes! Most certainly it would be wise on my part to take it," replied Hippolytus.

"Do you know my King, there is an established guideline of conduct among humans?"

Hippolytus inquired, "What is this code of conduct you intend to talk about?"

"Humans hate the one who is haughty at heart."

Hippolytus agreed, "Yes, you are right. Haughtiness of heart breeds dislike among mortals."

Attendant said with a smile, "….And affability rears abundant charm."

"….And you stand to achieve rich gain with very little effort," nodded Hippolytus.

"Don't you think O King, that it is the same with the gods?"

"Stands to the reason, what holds good in our world, the same must hold good in theirs."

The attendant raised his point again, "Then, O King, how come you missed the salutation to the venerable goddess?"

"Whom did I miss? Beware of your words lest you err seriously," said Hippolytus with a stern countenance.

"You missed the other goddess that stands right in front of your house, the goddess Aphrodite."

Hippolytus cleared up, "I am chaste. I salute her from a distance."

The attendant again extended a word of caution, "Yet she is a venerable goddess in the entire mortal world."

Hippolytus clarified, "It is one's personal inclination to choose and honour one's revered god."

"May you be blessed! May you have as much sense you require," replied the attendant.

Hippolytus said, "A god that is worshipped during the night, is not my god."

Attendant, "In honouring the gods we must not be wanting."

Hippolytus, "Depart, my associates into the house. An elaborate supper awaits you on the table. Let me rub down my horses, mend them and set them to the chariot for exercise after the repast. And to you Aphrodite, I bid a long adieu."

The attendant addressed Aphrodite, "O sovereign goddess, the young men at times know not what they are saying. We adore your image, our mistress. You may pardon the ludicrous utterances from a young haughty tongue. You, being the goddess, are wiser than the mortals."

Aphrodite seemed to say, 'I am the goddess worshiped by men. And those who submit to me in all humility, I add to their honour. But for those, who are proud and assuming towards me, I pay them in their own coin. Gods are also pleased when honoured by humans. Hippolytus, the son of Theseus and Hippolyta, a pupil of the chaste Pittheus[12]says that I am the vilest of the deities, demeaning me as a nocturnal Goddess. He honours Artemis, the daughter of Zeus, counting her holiest of all Goddesses. For his blasphemous utterances, he will not be let go. I shall punish Hippolytus.'

~

Queen Phaedra

Theseus, the great Athenian hero and King, married Ariadne's[3] younger sister Phaedra. Phaedra was the Cretan[6] princess, daughter of Minos[10], Zeus's son and the King of Crete[6]. Phaedra's sister Ariadne was the Greek goddess of mazes and labyrinths. She was in love with Theseus, prior to his marriage with Phaedra.

Daring and adventurous, Theseus undertook hazardous journeys, slaying dangerous beasts and bandits on Earth and the underworld before he became the King of Athens. Theseus had married several times, with his last marriage being with Phaedra.

During his reign, the Amazons, race of the dreaded and the fierce warrior maidens, attacked Athens. In the battle that ensued, Theseus was attracted to their queen Hippolyta[8]. After defeating her in a hand-to-hand combat, he forced upon her. She subsequently gave birth to their son Hippolytus and died soon after.

~

Queen Phaedra is lying in her bed. She has eaten no bread for three days. Her beautiful face looks gloomy, pale and insipid with sickness. Her spirits are low. Her condition leaves her attendants guessing, 'What has happened to the queen? Has she been given bad news brought by the sailors? Or has her husband, the noble King, been lured by some other woman putting her to deep distress? The Queen appears deeply tormented, talking incoherently. Perhaps, there is some physical ailment or suffering that she doesn't reveal.'

Her favourite old nurse and confidante supports Phaedra to be out of her chamber in her bed.

The nurse said wearily, "The sickness of humans is a horrid thing. I am bewildered as to what I should or shouldn't do to bring relief to you. I have brought the couch, on which you have been tossing in fever out in the fresh air. But, soon you would be eager to go back in your chamber. There is no breather for you anywhere. You keep searching for something else. It is better to be sick than to attend to the sick. Illness is the single malady for the sufferer, but nursing the sick means the disquiet of the mind with exertion of the hands. I see that the entire human life is filled with misery. We are lured by what glitters on Earth and it remain elusive. We are carried away by the otiose, idle stories."

Phaedra screamed, "O attendants, lift my head to be upright. The joints of my limbs are becoming numb. The dressing over my head is heavy to wear. Take it off my head to free my hair. Let them fall on my shoulders."

The nurse fondly said, "Be courageous my child. Do not keep tossing your body restlessly. Try to be quiet. It will help you bear your sickness. Be patient, we mortals have to undergo misery at some point of our lives."

Restive Phaedra babbled the trail of thoughts crossing her mind, "I wish I could draw from the dewy fountain and drink pure waters resting under the lush leafy poplars. Take me to the mountains, in the woods full of pine trees where hounds and hunters chase the spotted stags. I intend to throw loud cheers to the hounds holding Thessalian javelin, with its steel tip close to the tresses over my ears, ready to hurl."

Nurse tried to allay her, "O my child, please do not babble deranged words in front of those here. Why do you carry such a craving for hunting? Why do you long for fountain steams, when there is fresh water close to you?"

Phaedra said, "O Artemis, the mistress of Salt Lake, of racing horses. I might find myself taming your Venetian colts."

Nurse sweetly scolded, "Why, in the name of God, my child you rattle senselessly? At one moment, you long to go to the woods hunting for wild beasts, but then you also want to go to the mountains. And now you desire for horses. Your utterances need an adept prophecy to reveal as to who of the gods is tormenting you and drifting you from your sanities."

Phaedra ventilated as if guilty of something, "I feel like a pariah for what I have committed. I have wandered away from my good sense. I have strayed. It is by the prompting of some God that has led to this fall. I am ashamed of my words. Cover my face, for I can't face myself. Tears are trickling down my eyes."

Nurse grimly said, "I will cover you up. But when will death cover my own body? The length of my life has taught me many things. My inference by far is that one must learn to toe the middle path in life in matters of love and friendship… Neither to remain too close nor too far. Nothing in extreme, so that the fall out of pleasures and pains get allayed."

The senior attendant asked the nurse, "O dear grand old lady, you are the faithful nurse of Queen Phaedra. She is in a much-tormented state. May we know from you, the cause behind the queen's ailment?"

The nurse replied in dismay, "I made an earnest inquiry from her. But she doesn't come out."

The attendant insisted, "Not even, what the origin of her spasms is?"

"My answer remains the same, 'she doesn't reveal'."

The attendant enquired, "How feeble her figure has become? She looks so pale and frail."

"Yes, she has kept food away for the past three days."

"Looks like her endeavour to invite her death."

The nurse said in a bit worked up tone, "Invite her death? She is starving herself to death."

"This is an abnormal situation. Does her husband know and approve of this?"

The nurse replied, "Where is her husband? He remains on move. Whenever he is around she conceals her feelings and says that she is not sick."

"But is he not able to read her state through her face?"

"He isn't here at this moment. He is away in the foreign lands."

The attendant insisted again, "You must urge the Queen to speak out about her disease and of her wavering senses."

"I tried many ways but without any headway. I have not given up and shall keep trying. I am always loyal to my mistress even in her calamity. You are witness to it."

The nurse signaled the attendants to move away. As they moved out of sight, the nurse continued to cajole the queen, "My child, if your disorder is unmentionable to your women attendants, I may call for a physician to help you out. But, your silence will not get you any remedy. Let me be candid with you, if you die you will betray your own children who might lose their share in their father's palace. The son of warlike queen of Amazon, Hippolytus, will become their master."

Phaedra suddenly jerked her head blaring, "Ah!"

Nurse exclaimed, "So, this touches you!"

Phaedra harshly, "For heaven's sake I entreat you not to speak about this man."

"This brings you to senses. But your mere concern will neither help your children, nor serve your own life."

Phaedra said emotionally, "I love my children but there is another storm of misfortune awaiting me."

Nurse raised her eyebrows, "I hope, my child, there is no stain of blood on your hands!"

"My hands are clean but my heart is stained."

"Has King Theseus sinned against you?"

"No! But I should also be guiltless in his eyes," replied Phaedra with eyes downcast.

"You are hiding something grave, which is goading you to die."

"It is for my good to remain silent and suffer."

The nurse was emboldened with the queen's utterances, "Are you in love, my child? Who is the man?"

"There is a man…..whose mother was an Amazon…," Phaedra faltered in her speech.

"You mean Hippolytus?" asked the nurse in daze.

"You have spoken the name, not I," said Phaedra in a low tone.

"What is this you have just said? This prompts me to death. This is a curse to daylight. I will push myself down the cliff. Luring the chaste and restrain people to fall in such evil love is unfair. Aphrodite is no goddess, who destroyed both my mistress and me."

Phaedra lamented, "Often in the long dark nights I have pondered, how the life of mortals gets adrift. Although we are able to discriminate between the right and wrong, yet we are not always able to practice the right, for our weakness for pleasure against virtue. In my case, after I was battered by love, I reflected upon how best I could endure it. I chose to be silent first, to conceal it. Then I tried to subdue my love with my chastity. But, by all these means I wasn't able to douse the fire ignited in me by Aphrodite. Best course then for me, I thought, was to embrace death leaving no dispute. My virtues are well known, but there were no witnesses to my wrongs. I was careful being a woman, I am more vulnerable and an easy object of hate. At least, I am happy that I am true to myself. There are women who pretend to be chaste in public but act lasciviously when in private. O Aphrodite, how could such women look directly into the eyes of their men? Such an idea itself sends a chill down my spine, that if it is ever discovered that I have disgraced my husband and my children. But, if I am drifted today from the path does my husband, the mighty King, not be made accountable in equal terms. Why am I seeking love outside my marriage?... Yet I feel that the time holds a mirror to all humans showing them occasional evil doers, I should not be seen among them."

Nurse after she calmed down said, "My mistress what you told me just now was so sudden that it frightened me. But that was, for me, a moment of my weakness. In the world of mortals, I feel, the second thoughts are wiser. In hindsight, your case does not appear so extraordinary. There are many who suffer like you, both men and women. Men however easily get away, but women are a convenient prey. The anger of a goddess of love led to your fall. It is not possible for us mortals to withstand the fury of the goddess Aphrodite. She is the one who sows the seed of desire, and we procreate. So put all evil thoughts and feeling of guilt at bay from you. No one is expected to be perfect in this mortal world. If you have more good than bad, you can count yourself to be better off being a mortal," the nurse continued, "You are in love, my child, endure it as it is the will of a god. Try to get over your illness by some good means."

Phaedra still asserted, "You articulate very well. Your enticing words destroy well-governed cities and homes. They are mellifluous to the ear but take away a listener's honour as time unfolds."

"Why do you pontificate? You do not need the ornamented words but a man! Let us be frank and talk about your pain. I would not have persuaded you for the sake of lust or your pleasure, if your life was not at stake."

"Oh you have spoken such evil words. Hold your tongue. Don't repeat these immoral words again," retorted Phaedra vehemently.

Nurse replied patiently, "Immoral they may be. But, they are better than sentiments loaded with mortality. A deed is better that saves your life, than one which brings you to a triumphant end."

Phaedra persuaded, "I beseech you, for God's sake do not proceed further. Your well-phrased utterings will be ruinous. You are not going to tell this to the son of Theseus."

Nurse nodded, "Don't worry my child. I shall arrange the matter honourably."

(There is sound of movement in the corridors adjacent to the queen's chamber. Hippolytus and his men appear to be around. The nurse moves out. Phaedra comes puts her ear to the door to eavesdrop the conversation between the nurse and Hippolytus.)

Phaedra directed her attendants, "Women, be silent!"

Attendant asked, "What is happening outside, mistress?"

"Hush! Let me hear the voices."

"I am silent," said her attendant.

Phaedra got nervous as she listened to the conversation, "I have lost! Women, you may also hear for yourself the noise coming through the door. Hippolytus is raising his voice on my nurse. She has destroyed me by revealing my unhappy state to him. She is my doctor but now her medicine has aggravated my illness and made my condition fatal."

The attendant looked alarmed, "What is the solution my mistress?"

"There is only one and that is the death. Only death can bring an end to my misery."

(Voices coming from outside become louder and clearer.)

Hippolytus in a high-pitched voice, "O mother Earth! O Sun! O blue sky! What abominable words are these I have to bear with?"

"Hush, my son, lest someone hear what you say."

Hippolytus continued in flustered voice, "Is it possible for me to swallow such obnoxious things in silence?"

Nurse knelt, "I beg earnestly by your beauteous hand, to keep my words with you."

Hippolytus said bitterly, "Don't bring your hand close to me! Don't touch my cloak!"

"I beg at your feet… please do not destroy me," the nurse supplicated.

"Do you mean you have not spoken anything evil?"

Nurse is shaken, "Yes, my son, but what I narrated to you is not for everyone."

"Why not?" thundered Hippolytus.

"O, my child, do not break your oath."

"My tongue has sworn, but my mind remains unsworn," Hippolytus gave a bewildered look.

"My son, what will you do? Will you destroy your own friends?"

"Friends?" shouted Hippolytus, "Could a vicious person ever become my friend?"

"Pardon me, my child, a human is not infallible."

Hippolytus poured his sorrow, "O, Lord Zeus why did you place women in this world? If you wished to propagate the race of mortals, there was no necessity to do it through women. The men may have dedicated gold, bronze or iron in your temples and bought sons, for consideration of worth paid by them. Houses could have remained free of the blemished presence of women. Now we have to inherit this evil to erode the fortune of our homes. What bigger proof for their evilness is needed that a father who begets her, raises her up, rids her to another home adding gifts and dowry. The husband whom she joins is lucky if she is dim witted and is useless, for her simplicity. I hate the wily women with more gifted minds. Aphrodite conveniently uses the minds of the clever ones to breed the mischief. Now, in our home, the mistress devised a mischief and her attendant took it further. O you wretched woman, without a second thought you dared to come to me to share my father's bed. It is my goodness that you have been spared. Had I not been taken unaware by an oath I would not have refrained telling these sinful things to my father," stepping away Hippolytus continues, "Now, I will leave this house and remain away until Theseus returns from a foreign land. I will remain silent but will keep a close watch on you and your mistress. I have swallowed your daring notoriety with a curse on you both."

(As Hippolytus exits, the nurse walks into the queen's chamber.)

Phaedra is lost in her thoughts, 'What rancorous destiny does a woman have? Where can I escape from my destiny? Which of the gods or even humans will hold my hand knowing my misdeeds. I have reached the limit of my sufferings. I am the most ill-fated woman of all.'

Nurse with an expression of dejection said, "I am terribly sorry mistress. I have failed in my ploy. I has been calamitous."

Phaedra remarked sarcastically, "What a great service you have rendered to your mistress. May Zeus, my ancestor, uproot you from the world. I cautioned you not to air a word, but you went ahead and that afflicts me now. You did not hold yourself back in your misjudged adventure and now I cannot even have a dignified death. Hippolytus's anger has been heightened. He will expose all the wrongs to his father and that will decry me on this land. May you perish the way I will be destroyed."

Nurse dismally said, "Mistress, in your spell of sorrow, you may pass the entire blame on me for my failings. However, I am your loyal servant who has brought you up with my complete affection. I made an earnest attempt to relieve you of your love-sickness. Had I succeeded I would have been ranked as the wise one. Our wisdom is rated according to our failure or success."

Phaedra agitated, "What kind of conduct is yours? First you unveil a fatal blow and then argue with me on its merits."

Nurse continued to assuage, "My child, we have talked for too long now. I accept that I did not behave wisely but, I feel, you can still circumvent this scandalous quagmire."

"Do not speak to me anymore. I need no more advice from you. Move away from my sight and attend to your own affairs, leaving me alone. I will handle this myself."

(Nurse leaves the chamber.)

Phaedra addresses the attendants, "You noble women of Troezen, promise me that what you have heard remains with you."

The attendants' leader said, "We swear by the holy Artemis, daughter of Zeus, that we will never share the predicament with anyone."

Phaedra in a softened tenor, "I am grateful to you women. I have found at least one solace in this calamitous situation that I fade away without a blemish on my name. There will be no shame for my children and my Cretan house. Nor shall I face Theseus on the hideous charge on my head that I acted basely."

The attendants' leader enquired with suspicion, "May I know from you mistress, what desperate deed you are contemplating to commit to get out of this mess?"

Phaedra in a plain voice, "To die. But with a careful plan."

The attendant gets startled, "Mistress, do not venture out such an ominous thing."

Phaedra continued, "I shall fall silent. But, with my getting off this sullied life I shall enchant the goddess Aphrodite who destroys me. In my death, at least, I shall bring agony to another who has an immodest heart. He will not be able to smile arrogantly at my ruin. This will teach him a lesson."

(Attendant bows and exits.)

Phaedra sitting alone pondered, "Under the spell of Aphrodite, whom we revere as goddess, my willpower has been shattered. Alas! I am diseased by impious love. I am engulfed by the surge of misfortune. The only passage for me is a noose around my neck and hang myself from the ceiling of my bridal chamber. Though shameful, but this appears to be an honourable exit. And I choose that."

~

Queen's Self-Destruction

(There is commotion inside the Queen's chamber. Loud voices are emanating from the chamber.)

Nurse shouted in panic, "Is anyone listening? Help! Our mistress has hanged herself."

The attendants' leader rushed and stood in shock, "Oh! Queen suspended from the noose, she is no more!"

Nurse cried, "Rush! Bring a knife immediately to cut the rope."

(The knife is brought. The noose is severed. She is lowered and laid, pulling her limbs straight. It is too late. The queen has stopped breathing.)

An attendant was heard announcing outside, "Women, the King has arrived."

(Theseus enters in the corridor.)

Theseus enquired, "Women, what is this clamour in my house? Isn't it strange that after returning from a long trip no one is there to open gates for me? As if, I am not welcomed in my own house. Is there a bad news awaiting me? Is my old father alright?"

Attendant replied, "Master, it is not the old but the young who is dead. Sadly, that will make you grieve."

Theseus gave a bewildered look, "Is it one of my children, snatched away from me?"

"They all live, O King. But their mother is dead."

Theseus in disbelief, "This cannot happen! My wife? How could she be dead?"

Attendant in a feeble voice, "She tied a noose around her neck."

Theseus anxiously asked, "What had been her sorrow? Was it due to her loneliness or a sudden calamity?"

"I am also unaware, master. I have also just entered the house."

Theseus lamented, "Alas! Alas! Why this coronet sits over my head? My journey has ended in misery. Open the door. Let me have the sight of my wife. She has killed me in her own death."

(The door of the queen's chamber is opened. Phaedra's corpse is lying. Theseus enters the chamber.)

Theseus mourned bitterly, "I am consumed by sorrow. Nothing but sorrow. O, cruel hands of destiny you have shaken the very foundation of my house. Some evil spirit seems to have taken revenge. It has eroded my life completely. I have fallen into the sea of misfortune, struggling with the waves of calamity. My dear wife flew off my hands like a bird into the world unknown. It looks as if it is requital of old sins committed by my ancestors, which I am paying for now."

The attendant said, "Calm down, O noble King! You aren't the only one who has faced such peril. There are many other like you who lost their gracious wife."

There is no effect of the attendant's comforting words. The King continued to cry at his grave loss, "There is darkness beneath the Earth. You have moved to the underworld in search of happiness. You, my most loved companion, your death is more like mine. How did this misfortune strike your heart? Will anyone tell to me what all happened to her? What for you host of attendants flock my palace if you can't explain?... I am completely undone. My children have become orphans without you."

(Attendants get teary with emotion. They jitter with the fear, for more misfortune awaits the house.)

"What is this letter fastened to her hand? Does she want to convey something?" Theseus continued as he saw a sealed letter in Phaedra's fist.

(Attendants anxiously witness as Theseus breaks the seal and goes through the letter.)

The attendants' leader prayed, "I foresee a bigger calamity awaiting. O God, if you care to listen, save this house from destruction."

Theseus bemoaned reading the letter, "My trail of sorrow is endless. It is beyond words, beyond my endurance."

Attendant asked, "Master! What is the matter? Do share with us if it can be."

"The letter cries aloud! It wrings the death bell. I am perished, completely destroyed."

The attendant was puzzled, "Your expression forebodes grievous trouble, master."

"Alas! What has been said in this letter can no longer be kept a secret sealed within my lips. Though it is abhorrent, yet I will speak aloud. My citizens, Hippolytus, my son, had forced upon my wife in my bed. He has committed terrible sin. O father Poseidon[13], once you had promised me three curses, now I exercise one of these. I pray to you to kill my son. If your promise is true, he should not live beyond this day."

The attendant, shocked on hearing the King's curse, cries, "O King! Withdraw your bane, lest you repent later, for your blunder. I make an ardent prayer to you."

"I will not recall my curse. I shall rather add another curse to banish him from this land if Poseidon does not send him dead to the underworld of Hades. By putting him into exile, I want him to wander as a beggar precariously in an alien land."

The attendant announced, "Lo! Your son has come. You may vent your fury O King Theseus the way you consider best for your house."

~

Father's Curses

(Hippolytus makes an entry with his men.)

Hippolytus giving a surprised look, "I heard the sound of wailing, father. There appears to be no reason for you to mourn. Oh! I see your wife, father. I can't believe, she is dead. What is the reason of her sudden death? I want to hear from you, father. When in misery, it is not the time to remain silent. You must share your misfortune with your friends and with those who mean even more."

"Humans have not grown beyond savagery. They may learn thousands of skills but one thing they do not get versed with, is to be humans with wisdom to discriminate between the right and wrong."

"The canny teacher would urge those who are without wisdom, to be wise. But, why talk at this hour, my father? It appears that your sorrow has made your tongue go astray," said Hippolytus.

Theseus threw sarcasm at his son, "If there were unfailing criterion available to make distinction between a true friend and a rogue, humans would have had two voices – one true voice and the other of an ingrate. We could then have easily discerned between the two and were never deceived."

Hippolytus catching the scorn in his father's tone said, "Has someone poisoned your ears against me? Do you suspect me of something? I am innocent, father. Your words amaze me. They are far from the truth."

"It is sad to see how far the mind of the human would go in its audacity. If the human viciousness goes on escalating, generation after generation where is it going to terminate. The gods will have to add another world to habitat such wicked souls," Theseus poured his injury in words, "Look at this fellow, who is my son has encroached upon my bed and is now tarnishing it. It is the dead's testimony that cries aloud, for him being a nasty disgusting wretch. With such perversity, how can you show your face to your father? You pretend to be a holy man with extraordinary chastity and purity. Who stands to believe your pompous boasts? You read thick volumes of books, but what purpose do they serve if they have no positive influence on you? You speak in sweet, edifying, tongue-rattling, sermonic words to elude simple souls, trapping them to meet your nefarious designs," Theseus continued, "My noble wife is dead. You might have thought that her death will save you. You assumed that you will prove yourself innocent pleading your case playing with clever words. But her body lying here outweighs all your arguments. I know that you will try to put accusations on her that she hated you to her bone. You would argue that women are prone to folly and that men are different. I know young men who do not remain even a bit more trustworthy than women when under the influence of Aphrodite on their youthful minds. But, their pretense of being 'male' acts a protective shield. But, why should I contest against your words when the dead woman speaks for herself? Leave from this land as early as possible. You are exiled. Never be seen in, the God built, city of Athens or wherever my empire extends. If I pardon you for your sin, people of my land would never believe my words that I never spared the evil doers whosoever he may be."

"Acrimony and rancor of your mind is terrifying. You articulated it well to make it convincing. But, if someone looks at it dispassionately, the truth in this matter will be laid bare. I, however, lack the skill to put facts into eloquent arguments to make them irrefutable. I assert that there is no man more chaste than me, though you may not agree at this moment," Hippolytus continued to plead, "I am culpable in your eyes father, but I may tell you in my plain words that I am pure not only in body but also in thoughts. I live with a spotlessly virgin soul. If you disbelieve, give me a reason. Was it that I strayed because she was beauteous of all the women around? Or was it by taking her to your bed I would gain this palace and kingdom in dowry? If I had thought that way there was no bigger fool than me. To me the monarchy is not alluring. I rather yearn for winning an athletics contest in Grecian games or prefer to live in an inviolable society in the company of my choicest friends. I shall add a few words before I end my defense. Since there are no witnesses whom you could cross-examine and she is not alive to cross-examine my contention, I swear by Zeus, the god of oaths, that I never touched your bridal bed nor even wished or thought of it. If I have done so, I may succumb, inglorious, nameless, homeless, stateless, as a beggar in exile. Neither sea nor earth should accept my body when I am dead, if I had even a faint streak of evil in me. And I may say, finally, that she took her life out of fear of getting exposed. She died as she was not chaste and the irony is that it is my chastity that has brought me to my wreck."

The attendants' leader, standing by the side, whispered to her companion, "Hippolytus has effectively rebutted the charges imposed on him, fortifying it by his oath in the name of god Zeus."

Theseus, however, remained unconvinced, "See this man who is beguiling me using his enchanting magical skills, to pacify my fury over the wrong he has committed to my wife and me."

"I wonder at your stance my father. If we could swap our positions, for if you were my son and I your father I would never banish you to exile. I would have preferred to kill you if I thought you had besmirched my wife."

Theseus became impatient, "Do you think that your glib argument is going to get you an easy end? I may tell you that you need not aspire for quick death for such an unforgivable crime. You will be wandering away in a foreign land in exile, facing the vagaries of life. This would be a befitting reward for your impious deed."

Hippolytus inquired, "Will you not even wait until the evidence against me proves me guilty? Should I walk away immediately to exile?"

"Yes, I would have thrown you beyond the seven seas that is the measure of my hate for you."

"Will you not care to examine my oath and my defense statement? So I stand banished without a fair trial?"

Theseus angrily retorted, "This letter is the biggest testimony against you. No further proof is needed to establish the truth."

"So now is the time for me to leave. Where shall I move from here? With such charges on my head, who will entertain me in his house?"

Theseus mocked, "Certainly, you will be well entertained by those who live by such evil deeds."

Hippolytus in emotional tenor, "The blow strikes me deep inside and makes me cry father. I have been adjudged a villain, by you who plays the judge and the jury."

"You should have cried and thought of it earlier, when you dared to wrong your father's wife."

Hippolytus looked around the walls of the mansion and said, "O, the high walls of this house if you could speak, your one voice could testify if I were a villain or not."

"You are trying your futile tricks through these witnesses and expect them side with you in your crime. They are also mute observers of your atrocious act," mocked Theseus.

"Alas! If I could stand outside me and look at my own face and the tears of my suffering."

Theseus mocked, "You are a narcissist, the self-possessed. This is the only thing you have mastered, but no other virtue."

"O! My unhappy mother, you had an unsavory labour pains to bring me on Earth and suffer as an illegitimate child," lamented Hippolytus.

Theseus directed his guards, "Drag him out of here! Guards, did you not hear it long time since I pronounced his banishment?"

Hippolytus ordered sternly, "Men, dare not touch me. You have such big desire, father, drive me out from this land yourself."

Theseus retorted, "I will resort to that too, if you do not obey my orders. There is no pity for your banishment in my heart."

(Theseus moves away with quick steps. Hippolytus goes out and stands opposite the statue of Artemis and opens the sorrow of his heart.)

"There is no escape for me now. I am doomed. My tongue is tied, and I cannot speak the truth. Thou, the dearest of deities to me, my compatriot and companion in hunt look at me, I stand banished from the great land of Athens. Adieu, O city, O plain of Troezen[15]adieu. You blessed me with a splendid time as a young man. Farewell! I look upon you for one last time and greet you.

My friends and fellow citizens I bid adieu to you. You shall never again see a man more chaste and restraint, though my father may not agree."

(Hippolytus exits.)

The sky, the sad witness, reverberates, 'I am aghast, a witness of what I never imagined. I see the brightest star of this land dismissed to alien lands, for his father's rage. He, with all majesty, will no longer mount on his royal chariot driven by the group of Venetian steeds resonating rhythmic clopping of their hoofs. The ceaseless melody of his cithara5 will fall silent in his father's house. No more maidens will pine for his love. But, I shall remain sad and teary for his condemnation without a hint of his fault. I am upset with the gods who did not intervene. Why they let him move far away from his land for no fault of his own?'

~

End of Hippolytus

The attendants' leader exclaimed, "Look! Hippolytus's attendant is coming along with a messenger with hasty steps. He appears to be in deep distress."

Messenger asked, "Women! Can I see King Theseus? Is he there in the palace?"

The attendants' leader, "Lo! The King himself is coming out."

The messenger spoke hastily, "Master! I am sorry; there is a sad news for you and for all those who live in Athens and in the realms of Troezen."

Theseus enquired, "What is it? Is there another calamity in a row?"

The messenger broke the news, "I'm afraid master, Hippolytus has died or I may say he is in a very grave condition. He may not survive for long."

Theseus asked, "Who killed him? For sure, someone whose wife he would have defiled as he did to me."

"The horses of his own chariot killed him. The curse from your mouth and your prayer to Poseidon proved fatal for him."

Theseus exclaimed, "O Lord Poseidon, my true guardian, you heard my imprecations! Tell me messenger, how did he die? In what manner did the staff of justice strike him as a reprised to my contempt?"

The messenger narrated to the King, "We were at the sea shore, combing and mending our horses. A horseman landed at the shore riding his swift horse, and broke the news that Hippolytus has been banished from this land. Then Hippolytus himself came, thronged by his myriad friends and companions, all in tears. Soon he restrained his emotions and spoke, 'Why do you all lament so much? It is my father's command, which I must obey. My companions strap my horses to the chariot, for this is not my city anymore.' The horses were made ready and brought before the master. He saddled himself and took the reins in his hands. Before he set out, he raised his hands to the sky and addressed the gods, 'Zeus, it is the time for me to die, if I were a wicked person. May my father realize that he did me wrong, whether I am gone or I live to see another day.' Then with a goad in his hand, he drove the horses to move. We all rushed behind the master's chariot as he took the reins and moved on the road that leads beyond this country. We followed him down the road and reached the shore of Saronic[14]Gulf. As we approached the lonely countryside there was a deafening sound that tore the sky. The horses raised their heads and their ears erected towards the sky with the sudden jolt. We all were stunned with fear and gazed in the direction from where the sound was emanating. We saw a mammoth sea wave raising its crest high up in the sky turning the coastline invisible to the eyes. The horses galloped with panic and started racing opposite to the shore. Master, who has been an expert with handling the horses pulled the reins to slow them down. The horses, scared by the sound, ran amuck pulling the chariot on the rolling terrain towards the cliff nearby. The wheel of the chariot suddenly struck a rock boulder. The impact was so heavy that the axle of the wheel and its pins gave way. Unfortunate for Hippolytus that he got entangled in the reins and was dragged with the rushing horses. He tried but could not untangle himself till his head pounded against the rocks. With bruises all over his body he cried aloud, 'Stop, horses stop! Do not kill me! Save me from my father's curse. I am a faultless, guiltless, true person. Save me!' We lagged behind not being swift enough. By the time we reached close to him we found him too feeble to breathe. The horses sped away and vanished in the horizon. O King, I am a mere slave in your house. But, it is beyond my imagination that your son was evil. He was a noble man."

Theseus remained unmoved, "I am pleased with your account, as I had deep hatred for the man who suffered. But since he was my son it neither makes me happy nor unhappy."

The messenger insisted, "If you permit master, I may bring him here. It is my submission to you; do not be harsh to your son, now that he is in moribund state."

Theseus nodded and responded in milder tone, "You may bring him here in front of my eyes. He vehemently refuted the charge that he defiled my bed. I may disprove him finally, for the fate he has met through the gods as punishment."

After giving his mind, Theseus pondered all over again as if goddess Artemis prompted him to rethink, 'The messenger's account puts me in the state of bewilderment. Was my conclusion that was solely based on my dead wife's testimony, just? In case I misjudged, then I have committed an irreversible blunder. If that be, where shall I go and hide my face? My grave indiscretion would be unpardonable.'

While Theseus lingered with his thoughts, the attendant appeared and addressed the King, "I may submit something to you master that your son was a man with a pristine heart. He has been slain, for the untrue words by your wife who was under a spell of infatuation with him. It appears to be the handiwork of Aphrodite whom Hippolytus offended through his neglect. Though Artemis, his revered goddess, would have tried to dampen the wrath of

Aphrodite but the goddess succeeded in putrefying the mind of the queen's favourite old nurse as well. The nurse's role in this affair was highly dubious who revealed her mistress's love for your son. But your son in his righteousness castigated your wife. The Queen was shocked and took the extreme step of taking away her own life out of fear of ignominy. To preserve her honour after death she wrote a suicide note, unfortunately containing lies. She succeeded in getting your noble son killed."

Theseus deeply repented, "Oh! Such terrible folly!"

Attendant poured further, "O King! This remains even more tormenting because your son rendered his version to you under the oath of father Zeus, which was overlooked by you. A dead person's testimony outweighed the living person's oath. You invoked your curse against your son, in haste, without examining the facts and he suffered terminally."

Theseus bemoaned, "I am finished!"

(Hippolytus is brought inside supported by his attendants.)

Hippolytus whined with the pain in his battered body, "Ah! Men, please handle with soft hands. Pain in my limbs and joints is unbearable. Gods be merciful with me! Oh father your curse has been lethal. Death only can be of some relief."

"So unfortunate! The nobleness of your heart became a curse for you," said the attendant desolately.

Hippolytus, with a feeble smile, exclaimed, "I feel a pleasant fragrance in the air. My pain has been softened. It appears that my benign goddess Artemis is around."

The attendant with a somewhat relieved look, "Oh! She is the most beloved goddess to the unhappy man."

Hippolytus said, "She is watching me in this state."

"Yes but the gods are refrained from shedding tears," said the Attendant.

"Alas! It is Aphrodite who destroyed the three lives," said Hippolytus.

"Yes, you, your father and his wife."

"I am even more sorry about my father. How misguided he was! He will have to live with this burden."

Theseus in a chocked voice, "There will be no happiness in my life hereafter."

"Father, now I see your sorrow has grown bigger than mine."

"Yes my son, it was I who should be dead instead of you."

"Father Poseidon's boons to you turned out to be banes to you."

"I wish they had never rolled out of my mouth,"

"You were so angry at that moment that you would have slain me even without them, father."

Theseus sighed, "The gods clouded my power of discrimination and my judgment."

"I wish, if mortals had the power to curse the gods."

"Sadly yes, my son! But to recompense for these tragic happenings I bestow great honours of the land of Troezen upon you. The unwedded virgins before their day of marriage will cut their locks in your honour, for the endless years to come. They will sing songs in your reverence."

Theseus then clinched his son into his arms and cried, "Humans do err when they are blinded by the gods. Forgive me Hippolytus!"

"Curtain comes down. I am nearing the death gate!"

"Son, you are leaving me with my hands stained with your blood."

"No, be in comfort father, I free you from the guilt," said in his last breaths Hippolytus.

"My most dear son, how noble you have been!"

"Adieu, father forever, Adieu!"

Chorus on the lips of Athenians pouring their sorrow:

'This common grief befallen on all the citizens,

Torrent of tears engulfing us all;

As we hear the lamentable stories of your nobility,

More and more and more!'

Epilogue-III

Legendary Greek tales, like the epics from other civilizations, have close association with nature and depict various shades of human emotions. The Iliad of Homer is one of the oldest pieces of Greek literature strung together in rich, subtle and beautiful verses. The journey of Greek's ancient literature followed thereafter. Interestingly, the Greeks delineate their gods in their own reflection.

Greek theatre is also over two and a half millennia old. Plays in the genre of comedy and tragedy were performed in the sixth century BCE in Athens at religious festivals. In fact, Greek tragedy reached its most significant form in the fifth century BCE. The most acclaimed Greek tragedians were Aeschylus, Sophocles and Euripides. Born in Attica, around 485 BCE, Euripides was the youngest of the three. There are over eighty plays associated with Euripides. He came from a well to do family, to spend his entire life without having to work for anything but write plays. He dedicated his life to writing. He was among those chosen to take part in the annual tragedy themed play competitions at the festival, in Dionysus[7] on twenty-two occasions starting from 455 BCE. The first prize in these contests came to him in the year 441 BCE.

The play Hippolytus, like all other legends, has many versions and renditions, Euripides' one being the most popular. Euripides himself presented his Hippolytus in two forms, one quite different from the other. The tales of Theseus's life, the King of Athens and father of Hippolytus, encompass his many daring adventures across varied realms extending even to the underworld. The legend of Hippolytus is set nearly at the end of the King's life. Theseus married several women in his lifetime and Hippolytus was his son born out of a short liaison with Hippolyta, the leader of the Amazonian female warriors after he defeated her in a combat.

Phaedra, his young beautiful wife, was of royal lineage. Phaedra felt attracted towards the young and handsome Hippolytus. Phaedra's attraction towards her strikingly attractive stepson is a kind of instinctual love, of a lonely wife. She, however, remains temperate enough to not reveal, as she is aware of its forbidden nature. As her obsession with him grows, she comes under severe mental distress and starves herself attempting to end her life. She often talks incoherently, expressing her desire to ride a wild horse. Hippolytus, in Greek language, means 'the unleasher of horses'. Her behaviour is a cause of concern to her attendants and to her old nurse, her favourite. Upon repetitive coaxing, by her confidante nurse, Phaedra reveals her buried feelings towards Hippolytus. The nurse, intending to relieve her mistress of her agony conveys the queen's love to Hippolytus. Hippolytus, an open misogynist in his haughtiness, not only rejects but also becomes contemptuous for her.

Phaedra didn't want to risk her marriage, however was unable to grip her emotions. She knew that although Theseus committed adultery on several occasions, yet he would not approve of even the thought of his wife doing the same. Phaedra's expression, '…if I am drifted today from the path does my husband, the mighty King, not be made accountable in equal terms. Why am I seeking love outside my marriage? Yet I feel that time holds a mirror to all humans showing them occasional evil doers, I should not be seen among them,' is a testimony of her feelings. And she is aware that being a woman she is on an uneven footing as she says, 'I was careful being a woman, I am more vulnerable and an easy object of hate.' With fear of being disgraced, ultimately Phaedra killed herself.

The earlier version of the legend that Euripides composed was titled 'Hippolytus Veiled' in which he depicted Phaedra as a bold, brazen and outspoken woman who aired her desire to Hippolytus. Driven by the King's philandering nature she made sexual advances towards her stepson. Hippolytus, in this version, is portrayed as an innocent youth sickened by Phaedra's advances and out of shame covers his face with a veil thus getting the title *Hippolytus Veiled*. This version was rejected by the public since such sexually explicit behaviour of a Royal Queen was not comestible to them. Euripides lost the contest. He had to rewrite his tale making amends in order to present a milder version of Phaedra and show Hippolytus's acceptable character, a somewhat misogynist.

Phaedra appears a villain here. But on a closer second look, her story is about the destiny of a dissatisfied, miserable woman in marriage, devoid of love. Her adventurous husband Theseus remains away for months to foreign lands, as she sits waiting in emptiness. Phaedra is both a victim, and a victimizer. Hippolytus is a victim to the circumstances.

End Notes-III

1. Aphrodite: Goddess of love and beauty who beguiled all, gods and men alike. The laughter loving goddess who laughed sweetly or mockingly at those her wiles had conquered.

2. Apollo: The son of Zeus and Leto (Latona). He is known as most Greek of all gods. God of Light and Truth. Master musician who delights Olympus.

3. Ariadne: Cretan princess of Greek mythology. She was associated with mazes and labyrinths where sacrifices were made.

4. Artemis: Greek goddess of wild animals, hunting, vegetation and chastity. Daughter of Zeus and Leto and twin sister of Apollo. Identified by Romas as Diana.

5. Cithara: An ancient Greek and Roman stringed musical instrument similar to the lyre.

6. Crete: Largest and most populous of the Greek islands. First advance civilization of Europe from 2700 to around 1400 BCE.

7. Dionysus: Son of Zeus, the Greek god of wine, wine making, fertility, theater and religious ecstasy. The theater of Dionysus, one of the world's first theaters was built in his honour in ancient Athens. Both comedies and tragedies were performed at the large outdoor theater and were part of competitions.

8. Hippolyta: The queen of Amazons. Mother of Hippolytus.

9. Leto: Mother of twins Apollo and Artemis whom Zeus was the father.

10. Minos: The powerful King of Crete, son of Zeus and Europa in Greek mythology. The Minoan civilization of Crete has been named after him. The father of Phaedra from his wife Pasiphae.

11. Olympus: Mount Olympus was regarded as home to gods and the seat of Zeus in Greek mythology.

12. Pittheus: King of Troezen and father of Theseus's mother. Had the highest repute as man versed in lore of his times and of the greatest wisdom. Teacher of Hippolytus.

13. Poseidon: The ruler of the sea in Greek mythology. Zeus's brother and second only to him in eminence. He had a splendid palace beneath the sea but he was oftener to be found in Olympus.

14. Saronic Gulf: The gulf formed between the peninsulas of Attica and Argolis in Greece and is part of Aegean Sea.

15. Troezen: Birth place of Athenian hero Theseus. Small city in southeastern Argolis, Greece. According to the Greek mythology Troezen came into being as a result of the unification of the two ancient cities, Hypera and Antheia by Pittheus who named the new city in honour of his diceased brother Troezen.

16. Zeus: The king of gods. He is the Greek god of sky, the rain and cloud gatherer who wielded the thunderbolt. Roman equivalent Jupiter.

POTIPHAR'S WIFE

Characters-IV

JACOB : The patriarch of Israelites.

JOSEPH : Jacob's favourite son.

Joseph's eleven brothers.

RUBIN : The eldest brother of Joseph.

POTIPHAR : Captain of Pharaoh's guards.

POTIPHAR'S WIFE

CUPBEARER

CHIEF BAKER

PHARAOH

Joseph-The Beloved Son

Jacob, the patriarch of Israelites, had twelve sons by four women, his wives Leah and Rachel and his concubines Bilhah and Zilpah. Joseph was the only son born through Rachel, after being childless for a long time. As Joseph grew into a handsome young man of seventeen, he began to tend to the flocks with his elder brothers.

Born to Jacob, in his old age, Joseph was his father's favourite child. He made a specially crafted, ornate robe for him. Joseph was happy to get the beautiful robe from his father. When his brothers saw that their father loved Joseph more than the others, they developed hatred towards him and used to be rather unkind to him.

Joseph had a dream but when he narrated it to his brothers, their hatred grew further.

He said, "Listen to the dream I had. We were binding sheaves out in the field, when suddenly my sheaf rose and stood upright, while your sheaves gathered around mine to bow down to it."

Irked with what Joseph said, his brothers retorted, "Do you intend to reign over us? Will you rule us?"

Few days later, Joseph had another dream. He said, "Listen! I had another dream, and this time the sun and the moon and eleven stars were bowing down to me."

The sun and the moon symbolised his parents, and the stars denoted his brothers. The two dreams in which he was painted as ruling over his brothers heightened their jealousy. They became furious and shouted on him, "Shut up! We are not interested in your dreams."

Joseph quietly heard them shout on him as it wasn't his nature to contest in a petty manner.

~

Joseph, Sold By His Brothers

Joseph's brothers had gone to graze their father's flocks near Shechem [8] , the first capital city of the kingdom of Isreal. Jacob said to Joseph, "As you know, your brothers are grazing the flocks near Shechem, you must also go and join them."

"Very well, father," he replied.

The father further instructed his son, "Go and see if all is well with your brothers and with the flocks and bring your word back to me."

Then he sent him off from the valley of Hibron [5] .

When Joseph arrived at Shechem, a man found him wandering about in the fields and asked, "What are you looking for?"

He replied, "I am looking for my eleven brothers. Can you tell me where they are grazing their flocks?"

"They have moved on from here," the man answered, "I heard them say, 'Let's go to Dothan.'"

Joseph went searching for his brothers and found them near Dothan. His brothers saw him from a distance and their jealousy surfaced. Before he reached closer to them, they plotted to kill him.

"Here comes that dreamer!" they said to each other, "Come now let's kill him and throw him into one of these cisterns and declare that a ferocious animal devoured him. Then we'll see what comes of his dreams."

Reubin, the eldest brother, was somewhat considerate thought of rescuing him from others. "Let us not take his life," he said, "Don't shed any blood. Throw him into the cistern, here in the wilderness, but let's not lay a hand on him." Reubin secretly planned to rescue Joseph and take him back to their father.

As soon as Joseph arrived, closer to his brothers, they stripped him of the ornate robe he was wearing and tossed him into the cistern saying, "Let us know if you had this in your dream!" Lucky for Joseph, the cistern was empty with no water in it.

As they sat to eat their meal, they looked up and saw a caravan of Ishmaelites [6] coming from Gilead [3] . Their camels were loaded with spices, balms and myrrh and they were on their way to transport them to Egypt.

Judah, another brother of Joseph had an idea. He proposed, "What will we gain, if we kill our brother and cover up his blood? Come, let's sell him to the Ishmaelites and not lay our hands on him; after all, he is our brother, our own flesh and blood."

His brothers seeing no harm in it readily agreed.

So, when the Ishmaelite merchants came closer, his brothers pulled Joseph up out of the cistern and sold him for twenty shekels of silver to the Ishmaelites who took him to Egypt.

The eldest one got worried as to what reply they would give to their father, about Joseph's whereabouts. Then they planned and slaughtered a goat and dipped his robe in the blood. They took the ornate robe to their father and said, "We found this on our way back. Examine to see, whether it is Joseph's robe."

Father looked at the robe closely. He recognised that it was the robe presented by him to his beloved Joseph. In a state of shock he lamented, "It is my son's robe. Some ferocious animal appears to have devoured him. Oh! This is my son's blood!" Saying this he hugged the robe and cried inconsolably. Joseph's brothers feigned their sorrow and joined in their father's grief.

Jacob mourned the death of his son for many days. All his children came one by one to comfort him, with no avail.

"No," he said, "I have no respite. I will continue to mourn till I join my son in the grave."

~

Joseph, Auctioned To Potiphar

After a couple of days of travel, the caravan of merchants reached at the borders of Egypt. They brought Joseph to the slave market for auctioning. Egypt had thriving slave markets. The merchants made Joseph stand in the centre of a raised podium in front of the large gathering of buyers. The leader of merchants standing on the rostrum announced, "Here is this young man available to be at your service. He will go to the highest bidder. Minimum reserved selling price for this good-looking man is eighty shekels."

Bidders were attracted towards the well-built, handsome Joseph. The first bidder proposed, "One hundred shekels!"

The second bidder immediately raised the bid price, "Two hundred shekels!"

After a few moments of silence, there was a deep baritone voice from behind the crowd, "Three hundred shekels."

"Who is he?" asked the seller looking in the direction of the voice.

"It's me!" the elegantly dressed bulky statured Potiphar came forward. Everyone respectfully moved aside to make the way for him.

"Anyone else wants to raise on that?" called out the auctioneer.

Finding no further response from the crowd, the auctioneer announced, "Three hundred once! Three hundred twice! Three hundred final!"

With the drop of the hammer, Joseph was sold. The auctioneer happily handed over the young slave to Potiphar who had paid a good price.

Potiphar was one of the senior officials, the captain of Pharaoh's [7] guard.

He asked his newly acquired slave, "What is your name?"

"Joseph is my name, Master," replied Joseph politely.

Pleased with his looks and good manners, Potiphar said, "Don't worry Joseph you will be taken care of."

Potiphar brought him to his fields first. For some time, things began to look up for Joseph. Working diligently, he made a very positive impression on his co-workers and on his master. Very soon, he rose to become the head of Potiphar's estate. Joseph succeeded in every assignment he was allocated to. Potiphar's estate grew and he believed that Joseph had brought luck to him.

Potiphar called Joseph and lauded him saying, "I am quite pleased with your services and your honesty. We have fantastic growth this year. Now you will be in charge of my household in addition to my estate."

Joseph kneeled and said, "As you wish Master. All this is with the blessings of God."

Joseph moved to his Master's large mansion. Potiphar's demanding responsibilities with Pharaoh left little time at his disposal for himself. Therefore, everything Potiphar owned was entrusted to his care. With trustworthy man in charge of his personal farm and household, Potiphar was free to concentrate on the Pharaoh's duties effectively.

~

Joseph And Potiphar's Wife

Joseph was the man with a Midas touch. Wherever he laid his hands, it flourished. And Potiphar, with the focus on the Pharaoh's duties, further grew in his rank. Being a big food lover, he had only one task at home; to eat good food.

Potiphar had a young beautiful wife. Potiphar was too preoccupied with his job to spend time with her. She lived in plenty but without company. Like the wives of most aristocrats, she was fashionable and full of vanity. She would sit long hours in front of the mirror engrossed watching her own beauty. Potiphar being part of Pharaoh's entourage remained out with him for many days. During the initial days of their marriage, she would attire herself up in best of her apparel and jewellery to welcome her husband on his return. But to her dismay he remained unmindful to take even a good notice of her beauty. This was quite hurting to her.

Joseph the in charge of Potiphar's household, had to move around his Master's mansion supervising his daily chorus. Potiphar's wife took notice of this charming young man one day. She was captivated by his good looks and clandestinely watched him. Her eyes followed him whenever he was around. Joseph however remained too engaged with his work to take a notice of someone watching him. He kept himself limited to customary greetings to his Master's wife. However, her infatuation with Joseph grew with each passing day.

One day when no one was around, she called out, "Joseph! Joseph..."

Joseph looked about and saw the lady of the house standing behind the ajar door of her chamber looking at him. He walked over to her and asked reverentially, "Yes ma'am! What can I do for you?"

"Come inside Joseph," she said.

After a moment of hesitation Joseph said, "What is the matter?"

She simply gave a deep alluring smile. Joseph was too small a man to receive this kind of welcoming treatment form the high woman. He silently looked towards the lady, remaining motionless. Seeing him hesitate she gestured with her hand from behind the door inviting him to come inside. Somewhat alarmed Joseph mumbled, "I have been given an important task by the Master. Sorry, I beg your leave."

Joseph walked away with quick steps. She kept looking at Joseph as he vanished into the distance. She mulled over, 'Maybe Joseph felt shy!'

Potiphar's wife had all material comforts but loneliness was haunting her. Her husband made every possible thing available to her except his time and company. She kept daydreaming about Joseph.

~

The days rolled by. Potiphar's wife continued to watch him at times secretly, other times passing him instructions when he was with other attendants. Her gestures remained enticing towards Joseph. Joseph, however remained glued to his duties. One day, when no one else was around, she saw Joseph passing by her chamber. She became excited and called him, "Come here Joseph."

He bowed to her saying aloud, "Yes ma'am."

"Shh...come inside, I need to talk to you," she said.

"Can't we talk here?" replied Joseph.

"No! No! Come inside the chamber," she said almost in a tone directing him.

This time Joseph reluctantly obeyed. He entered into her majestic chamber. "What is the matter?" he asked giving a bewildered look.

She said adding extra sweetness to her tongue, "Joseph I find that you always remain busy. You must take a break once a while."

"Master's duty is the service to the God, I rarely feel tired, ma'am," smiled Joseph for the first time.

"That's great Joseph! But I feel very lonely. My husband has no time for me and I am without any company."

Joseph said, "Ma'am our Master has plenty of official responsibilities. His hands are always full. He remains busy with many things."

"He is always preoccupied with something or the other. He may be performing host of things for his office but he doesn't care to do what I require," she said in a complaining tone.

"Ma'am, the Master has made everything in his capacity available for you," insisted Joseph.

"But he is not available for me and that is too hurting," she said in a raised voice and moved closer to Joseph. She did not want to miss the opportunity. Burning with passion, she held Joseph by his cloak said in a low hedonic tone, "Joseph! Come to bed with me!"

Joseph was stunned for few moments as she continued to coax him. On gaining his composure he said, "With me in charge, my Master does not concern himself with anything in the house. Master has not withheld anything from me except you, because you are his wife. He has placed his entire faith and trust in me. How could I do such a wicked act and sin against God?"

Finding that his words have no effect on her and she did not forbear, Joseph became perplexed. He tried to seize his cloak from her hands. She kept tightly holding it. Finding no other option Joseph ran out of her chamber leaving his cloak in her hand. Seeing him running out, she became nervous that he might reveal about the incident to Potiphar. Out of panic, she raised an alarm calling out her household servants. A few of the attendants working nearby rushed to her chamber hearing her shrieks.

She was shouting flapping Joseph's cloak in her hand, "Look this Hebrew [4] has been brought to us to serve us… And see what he did, he dared to come inside my chamber, grabbed me and forcibly tried to bed with me. I screamed for help. In fear, he ran away leaving his cloak beside me."

She kept the cloak beside her until her husband came home. As he entered, she cried to him, "That Hebrew slave you brought here entered my chamber and tried to take liberty with me. When I resisted and screamed for help he left his cloak beside me and ran out."

First Potiphar couldn't believe that Joseph could do such evil act, but then his cloak in her hand was a live testimony. The attendants also narrated whatever they had seen. His wife's words, 'This is how your slave treated me,' burned Potiphar with anger. Master immediately caught hold of Joseph and yelled, "I reposed so much trust on you. I took good care of you and what have you given us in return? I am ashamed to even believe that you indulged in such a devilish act. Your right place is in prison."

He was so furious that he did not lend his ear to Joseph's pleadings. Potiphar put him in prison where Pharaoh's prisoners were confined.

Joseph was a pure innocent soul, the invisible hand of destiny was again there to pull him out of his misery. For his disciplined behaviour and good conduct, he found favour in the eyes of the prison warden. The warden made Joseph in charge of all those held in prison and gave him the responsibility of the activities undertaken inside the prison. He was so dependable that the warden was not required to bother for whatever he delegated to Joseph. Things once again started looking up for Joseph.

~

The Cupbearer And The Baker

Some time passed in Egyptian prison. The chief cupbearer [2] and the chief baker [1] of the King of Egypt offended their master over an issue. The Pharaoh was angry with his two officials, and put them in the same prison where Joseph was confined. The prison warden assigned them to Joseph, who attended to them.

After they had been in custody for some time, each of the two men had a dream on the same night. And each dream bore a meaning of its own. When Joseph came to them the next morning, he saw that they looked dejected.

He asked the Pharaoh's officials, "Why do you look so desolate today?"

"We had dreams last night," they answered, "But there is no one to interpret them."

Joseph said, "Do not interpretations belong to the Lord? Dreams are His messages. Tell me your dreams."

The chief cupbearer narrated, "In my dream, I saw a vine in front of me, and on the vine, there were three branches. As soon as it budded, it blossomed. Its clusters ripened into grapes. The Pharaoh's cup was in my hand, and I took the grapes, squeezed them into the cup, and placed the cup in his hand."

"This is what it means," Joseph said to him. "The three branches represent three days. Within three days, the Pharaoh will lift your head and restore you to your position and you'll put Pharaoh's cup in his hand, just as you used to do when you were his cupbearer. But when all goes well with you, remember me and show me kindness. Mention me to the Pharaoh and get me out of this prison.

I was forcibly carried away from the land of Hebrews and, even here, I have done nothing to deserve this dungeon."

When the chief baker saw Joseph had given a favourable interpretation, he said to Joseph, "I too had a dream: On my head were three baskets of bread. In the top basket were all kinds of baked goods for Pharaoh, but the birds were eating them out of the basket on my head."

"This is what it means," Joseph said, "The three baskets are three days too. Within three days the Pharaoh will lift off your head and impale your body on a pole. And the birds will eat away your flesh."

Now the third day was the Pharaoh's birthday, and he gave a feast to all his officials. The chief cupbearer and the chief baker were summoned in the presence of officials. Meanwhile Pharaoh had deputed his officials to give him information about his two imprisoned officials, the chief cupbearer and the chief baker. While Pharaoh's spies had given a positive feedback on the cupbearer, everyone spoke negatively about the baker to the extent that he was a danger to the state. Pharaoh acted on the advice of his senior officials and restored the cupbearer to his position so that he could once again put the cup in his hand. But he impaled the chief baker, just as Joseph had interpreted.

The chief cupbearer happily held the cup in in his hand, however, forgot about Joseph.

~

Pharaoh's Dreams

Two years passed. This time Pharaoh had a dream. He was standing by the Nile, when out of the river there appeared seven cows, all sleek and fat. The cows grazed among the reeds. They were followed by seven other cows, ugly and gaunt. They stood beside fat cows on the riverbank. The ugly cows ate the sleek, fat cows. Then the Pharaoh woke up in the middle of his dream.

He fell asleep again, had a second dream; seven heads of grains, healthy and good were growing on a single stalk. After the, seven other heads sprouted, thin and scotched by the East wind. The thin heads of grains swallowed the healthy, full grains. The Pharaoh awoke finally at the break of the dawn.

During the day, his mind was troubled by the hangover of those dreams. He called for all the magicians and wise men of Egypt. The Pharaoh told them his dreams, but none could interpret them for him.

The chief cupbearer, watching all this, said to the Pharaoh, "Today I am reminded of a young Hebrew whom I met in prison. I told him my dream back then, and he correctly interpreted them. His readings were precise, and I was restored to my position."

The Pharaoh sent for Joseph and he was quickly released. As he was brought out of the dungeon, he became happy to breathe in the free air. He was given shave, and his clothes were changed and he was taken to appear before the Pharaoh.

The Pharaoh said to Joseph, "I had a dream that no one is able to interpret. But I have heard, that you possess the ability to decipher dreams."

He narrated his dream to Joseph.

Joseph pondered for a while, and said to the Pharaoh, "Your Excellency, the seven good cows are seven fruitful years, and the seven good heads of grains are also seven years of abundance. And the seven lean, ugly cows and worthless heads of grains signify the seven of years of famine. The seven years of scarcity will follow the seven years of fortune. And during the years of famine the years of fortune will be forgotten."

The interpretation appeared logical to the Pharaoh's mind. He decided to put Joseph in charge of the land of Egypt. As deciphered by Joseph next seven years plenty of grain was produced in the fields. He ordered to collect a fifth of Egypt's harvest during the seven years of abundance. People happily shared a fifth of their produce as tax. They could store enough grains during that time. This was kept as reserve to be used for the seven years of famine in Egypt, to save the country from ruin.

~

Joseph, The Viceroy of Egypt

The events that followed were on the same lines as interpreted by Joseph. The populace was saved from the harsh period of famine. He was revered as a saviour of the land, and the Pharaoh was very pleased.

The Pharaoh declared, "I hereby put you in charge of the whole land of Egypt. You are my Viceroy now."

The Pharaoh took his signet ring and put in on Joseph's finger. He got him dressed in the robes of fine linen, and put a gold chain around his neck. He had him ride in a royal chariot as his second-in-command, and people cheered before him shouting, "Make way!"

Thus, he put Joseph in charge of all of Egypt. Every one of the land bowed before him including his previous master Potiphar. Joseph kept no grudges against all those who tried to harm him including Potiphar's wife, as he believed that goodness begets goodness. Perhaps he understood the agony of a lonely, disgruntled wife.

Epilogue-IV

Stories from the Bible are interesting way to imbibe moral values right from the childhood days. Rather than taking a didactic route, one can read and learn through a biblical tale, just like any other story and remember its contents without extra effort.

This is nearly four millennia old life event that was recorded in the Old Testament. The episode envelops the interplay of myriad human emotions such as love and hate, devotion and waywardness, ambition and otherworldliness, mercy and cruelty in its warp and weft. It depicts that even in the most trying times of life, patience pays and it is human spirit that has the potential to soar above empyrean heights.

Here Joseph is a noble human being, so he naturally ends up being happy. Potiphar's wife, on the other hand is a wicked woman. But, the question remains whether she is that vicious.

The leitmotif of the event is about a bored housewife who is seeking moments of thrill in an extramarital relationship. Her husband holds a high position as Captain in the king's guard. His high remuneration enables him to live a life of plenty. His job, however keeps him preoccupied leaving little time for the household and for his wife.

An aloof, idle and restless wife, when sees a well-built, handsome young servant, gets attracted towards him. She is looking for an escape from the purposelessness and parchedness of her life. The Hebrew version of the Old Testament terms her husband as *saris* (means eunuch), which slyly suggests that he was eunuch. During those days, female slaves were available to their masters, so she took it that naturally the young slave should be subject to her whims as well.

In The Book of Genesis of the Old Testament, Eve was attracted to the forbidden fruit, which appeared pleasing to her eyes and she was lured into eating it. A few millennia later, Potiphar's wife was tempted to another forbidden relationship as her suppressed instincts were desperately seeking expression. For her pain of rejection and fear of her husband, she fabricated a story against Joseph who was sent to prison. While one feels bad for Joseph who suffered for a short duration, one finds that destiny works in mysterious ways. The punishment became a stepping-stone for the man of destiny to join the high rank ruling elite of Egypt. In the entire event Old Testament nowhere mentions the name of the woman. This reminds of a short movie titled 'Two' made in the year 1964 by Satyajit Ray, one of the greatest filmmakers of all time. This twelve minutes long movie without a spoken word has only two characters, one of the characters is a rich boy living in a mansion whereas the other one, a poor boy, was picked up by the filmmaker from a shanty located close to the shooting site. The boy who played poor boy's character was literally poor from an agricultural household. While we know the name the rich boy (Ravi Kiran now a man) the boy who played the role of poor boy remains unknown. Even a maestro like Satyajit Ray forgot to record his name. Similarly the Old Testament doesn't provide the name of Potiphar's wife and she is just known by the name 'Potiphar's Wife'.

Potiphar's wife, though nameless, is labeled as a notorious woman and what ultimately happened to her is not known. She, however, does not stand alone in the ilk of those who are allured to the forbidden fruit at some moments of life.

End Notes-IV

1. Chief baker: An officer responsible for matters overseeing the production daily bread and other baked goods. During ancient times, the job required a person of complete trust to hold this position for the service of nobility.

2. Cupbearer: Historically an officer of high rank in royal courts, whose duty was to pour and serve the drinks at royal table. On account of constant fear of poisoning due to plots and intrigues, a person must have been regarded as scrupulously trustworthy to hold the position.

3. Gilead: Mountainous region east of Jordan river situated in modern day Jordan.

4. Hebrew: A member of an ancient people living in what is now Israel and Palestine. According to biblical tradition they are the descendants of patriarch Jacob, grandson of Abraham.

5. Hibron: Palestinian City in the South West Bank, thirty kilometers south of Jerusalem.

6. Ishmaelites: Ishmaelites are the descendants of Ishmael, the elder son of Abraham and the descendants of the twelve sons and princes of Ishmael.

7. Pharaoh: Common title used for monarch of Ancient Egypt. The dynasty began in 3150 BCE and remained until Egypt was annexed by Romans in 30BCE.

8. Shechem: First capital of the Kingdom of Israel as mentioned in Hebrew Bible. It is now identified with the nearby site of Tell Balata in the West Bank.

SELECT BIBLIOGRAPHY

Asoka and the decline of the Mauryas, Romila Thapar

Hippolytus, Euripides

Hippolytus Veiled, Euripides

Loona in Gurumukhi, Shiv Kumar Batalvi

Mythology, Timeless tales of Gods & Heroes; Edith Hamilton

Pooran Bhagat in Gurumukhi, Quadar Yaar

The Holy Bible (Genesis), The New International Version